The Evident Connexion: Hume
on Personal Identity

The Evident Connexion

Hume on Personal Identity

Galen Strawson

OXFORD
UNIVERSITY PRESS

Great Clarendon Street, Oxford OX2 6DP

Oxford University Press is a department of the University of Oxford.
It furthers the University's objective of excellence in research, scholarship,
and education by publishing worldwide in

Oxford New York

Auckland Cape Town Dar es Salaam Hong Kong Karachi
Kuala Lumpur Madrid Melbourne Mexico City Nairobi
New Delhi Shanghai Taipei Toronto

With offices in

Argentina Austria Brazil Chile Czech Republic France Greece
Guatemala Hungary Italy Japan Poland Portugal Singapore
South Korea Switzerland Thailand Turkey Ukraine Vietnam

Oxford is a registered trade mark of Oxford University Press
in the UK and in certain other countries

Published in the United States
by Oxford University Press Inc., New York

British Library Cataloguing in Publication Data

Data available

Library of Congress Cataloging in Publication Data

Data available

Typeset by SPI Publisher Services, Pondicherry, India
Printed in Great Britain
on acid-free paper by
MPG Books Group, Bodmin and King's Lynn

ISBN 978–0–19–960850–8

1 3 5 7 9 10 8 6 4 2

To my mother

Preface

This is a book about Hume's views on the mind. Part 1 provides background in the form of some general remarks on Hume's philosophy.[1] Parts 2 and 3 are a revised and considerably expanded version of a paper delivered in 1999 at the Hume conference at the University of Cork in Ireland.[2] Part 2 examines the famous 'bundle' account of the mind that Hume put forward in Book 1 of his *Treatise of Human Nature*. Part 3 analyses Hume's no less famous partial repudiation of that account in the Appendix to the *Treatise*.

My analysis of Hume's problem in the Appendix, in Part 3 of this book, doesn't depend on anything in Part 2, in which, in addition to arguing that Hume doesn't think that the mind is just a bundle of perceptions (for one proof, see pp. 57–8), I argue that the bundle account of the mind doesn't involve any sort of denial of the existence of subjects of experience, and that Hume never claims that the subject of experience isn't encountered in experience. One can doubt or reject these controversial claims about Hume's view, or about his view at the time he wrote section 1.4.6 of the *Treatise*, and still accept the conclusions of Part 3. So too one can reserve judgement on the 'sceptical realist' account of Hume's overall position in Part 1 and still accept the main claims of Parts 2 and 3.

This book was essentially complete in 2003, but I lacked time to finish it. This turned out to be fortunate. I received some helpful advice and had a few more ideas in the years running up to 2011, the tercentary of Hume's birth, although I never had time to catch up on the literature on Hume on personal identity. The book may be judged too long—I often try to express the same point in more than one way—but I won't mind if the book manages to put a dent in the view that Hume thinks that the mind is just a series of 'perceptions'.

When I cite a work by someone other than Hume I give the first publication date or estimated date of composition, while the page

---

[1] It reworks and augments Strawson 2000a, and includes elements of Strawson 1989 and 2000b. For more on the 'sceptical realist' interpretation of Hume see Wright 1983; also e.g. Buckle 2001, Kail 2007b, Wright 2009.

[2] 'Hume on himself'. A version of this paper was published in a *Festschrift* for Ingmar Persson (Strawson 2001).

reference is to the published version listed in the bibliography. For Hume's *Treatise* I give a page reference to the Selby-Bigge and Nidditch edition followed by the paragraph reference in the Norton and Norton edition; thus a typical *Treatise* reference is '233/1.4.5.5'. For the first *Enquiry* I give the Selby-Bigge page reference followed by paragraph reference in the Beauchamp edition; a typical *Enquiry* reference is '163/12.34'. In the case of the principal relevant section of the *Treatise*, 'Of personal identity', Section 1.4.6, I refer to paragraph 7 (say) simply by '§7'. In the case of the *Abstract*, the Appendix, and the Introduction to the *Treatise*, I refer to their seventh paragraphs (e.g.) as 'Abs§7' and 'App§7' and 'Int§7' respectively. In the case of Hume's *Dialogues Concerning Natural Religion* I give two page references, the first to the Kemp Smith edition, the second to the Gaskin edition. When quoting I mark my emphases by italics, and the author's by bold italics.

Acknowledgements

I'm extremely grateful to Don Garrett for his detailed comments in 2003 on a draft of Parts 2 and 3 of this book; and to Abe Roth and Helen Steward, who also saw an early draft. I gave versions of the material in Part 2 as papers at Rutgers and Princeton in 2001, at NYU in 2004 and St Andrew's in 2009, and received a number of useful comments. I remember in particular—among those whose names I know, and those with whom I've corresponded—Sarah Broadie, Stephen Buckle, Jonathan Ellis, Harry Frankfurt, James Harris, Javier Kalhat, David Lewis, Béatrice Longuenesse, David Owen, Ingmar Persson, Julia Simon, Udo Thiel, John Wright and Dan Zahavi. I'd like to thank members of my classes at the CUNY Graduate Center (2004-5) and MIT (2010)—including in particular Katherine Dunlop, Aaron Garrett, Chris Howard, Jeremy Ginsburg, Leonard Katz, Peter Langland-Hassan, Fauve Lybaert, and Ryan Priddle—for help on one matter or another. At the Oxford University Press, my multivalent thanks go to Sarah Cheeseman, Eleanor Collins, Carla Hodge, and Peter Momtchiloff. I'm also most grateful to the British Academy and the Leverhulme Trust for awarding me a Senior Research Fellowship for the academic year 2009–10. I wasn't awarded the fellowship specifically to finish this book, but it turned out to be a necessary part of the work I had applied to do.

Contents

Part 3 Hume's Appendix

PART 1

Epistemology, Semantics, and Ontology

'the essence of the mind [is] . . . unknown to us'

Hume 1739: xvii/Int§8

If I examine the PTOLOMAIC and COPERNICAN systems, I endeavour only, by my enquiries, to know the real situation of the planets; that is in other words, I endeavour to give them, in my conception, the same relations, that they bear towards each other in the heavens. To this operation of the mind, therefore, there seems to be always a real, though often an unknown standard, in the nature of things; nor is truth or falsehood variable by the various apprehensions of mankind. Though all [the] human race should for ever conclude, that the sun moves, and the earth remains at rest, the sun stirs not an inch from his place for all these reasonings; and such conclusions are eternally false and erroneous.

Hume 1742: 164

1.1 The necessity of metaphysics

David Hume rebukes dogmatic metaphysicians who think they can achieve certainty about the ultimate nature of reality. Or rather, he rebukes those who think that we can achieve certainty about the ultimate nature of reality other than the reality of our 'perceptions' or *experiences*, our conscious mental goings-on considered just as such, i.e. just in respect of their conscious experiential character.[1] For he takes it that we can know the

---

[1] 'Nothing is ever present to the mind but its perceptions; . . . all the actions of seeing, hearing, judging, loving, hating, and thinking, fall under this denomination. The mind can never exert itself in any action, which we may not comprehend under the term of *perception*' (456/3.1.1.2).

ultimate nature of our perceptions or experiences, so understood.[2] 'The perceptions of the mind are perfectly known' (366/2.2.6.2); all we have to do is have them.

His rebuke is just, but one can't escape metaphysics altogether. For as soon as one admits that something exists—and one must do that—one has to admit that it has some nature or other. For to be is necessarily to be somehow or other—to have some nature or other. And as soon as one admits that what exists has some nature or other, one faces a choice. One can either hold that one knows what this nature is, and endorse a particular metaphysical claim about the nature of reality, or grant that one doesn't and perhaps can't know what it is; or at least that one may—perhaps must—have an incomplete picture of it.

The second option is the right one, but to deny the possibility of knowledge is not to deny the existence of facts. Even if one holds that one doesn't and can't know, or can only partially know, the ultimate nature of reality, other than the reality of one's experiences (considered just in respect of their conscious experiential character), one must grant that this reality has a certain nature, and *a fortiori* that it is meaningful or coherent to suppose that this is so. One must do this even if metaphysical speculation is fruitless. For, to repeat, something exists, and to exist—to be—is, necessarily, to be somehow or other: to have a certain nature.

Hume knows this—unsurprisingly, because it's obvious. His considered position, when it comes to substantive propositions about the ultimate nature of reality, is not that they're meaningless—entirely meaningless. It is that although they do have some sort of content, they're profoundly unsatisfactory from a philosophical point of view. Questions about their truth and falsity are radically undecidable, philosophically speaking, and are therefore a waste of time. All philosophical attempts at definite answers are 'sophistry and illusion' (163/12.34).

Speaking of our sensory experiences, Hume says in the *Treatise* that

their ultimate cause is, in my opinion, perfectly inexplicable by human reason, and 'twill always be impossible to decide with certainty, whether they arise immediately from the object, or are produc'd by the creative power of the mind, or are deriv'd from the author of our being.[3]

---

[2] I use 'experience' where Hume uses 'perception'.

[3] 84/1.3.5.2. Compare Newton's position on the *vera causa* (true cause) of the phenomena described by his laws: the *vera causa* is something real, of course, but it's unknown by us, and perhaps unknowable (Newton 1687: Definition 8).

To say this is plainly not to hold that the notion of an ultimate cause of our experiences is meaningless. He puts the same point in the *Enquiry* by asking a rhetorical question:

By what argument can it be proved, that the perceptions of the mind must be caused [as Locke supposes] by external objects, entirely different from them, though resembling them (if that be possible) and could not arise either from the energy of the mind itself [as the solipsist supposes], or from the suggestion of some invisible and unknown spirit [as in Berkeley's view], or from some other cause still more unknown [as in Kant's view]? (152–3/12.12)

His answer is that it can't be proved by any argument. It is, he says,

a question of fact, whether the perceptions of the senses be produced by external objects, resembling them.

That is, it's either true or false. It could be true, and so it's certainly meaningful. But it's radically undecidable, for

how shall this question be determined? By experience surely; as all other questions of a like nature. But here experience is, and must be entirely silent.[4]

The great Western flight from metaphysics culminated in twentieth-century verificationist positivism, but twentieth-century verificationist positivists didn't escape metaphysics. For even they granted that experiences certainly exist, just as Hume granted that experiences certainly exist. If verificationist positivists had gone on to say that experiences[5] are definitely all that exist they would have adopted a patently metaphysical position, one of the most remarkable on record, far stranger than Berkeley's. And the same would have been true of Hume, if he had adopted the view that experiences are definitely all that exist.

He does consider such a view. He points out, correctly, that if a substance is defined as a self-subsistent entity, i.e. an entity that doesn't depend on anything else for its existence—'*something which may exist by itself*' and has 'no need of anything else to support [its] existence'

---

[4] 153/12.12. Hume's assertion that it's a question of fact whether sensory experiences are caused by external objects is categorical. It's not qualified by the doubt he has just expressed about whether anything like Locke's resemblance claim could ever be true (Locke's claim that our ideas of primary qualities like extension and motion resemble or correctly depict primary qualities as they actually are in objects). See further Wright 1983: ch. 2, Strawson 1989: 50n, 51n.

[5] Or 'sense-data', understood as mental entities.

(233/1.4.5.5)—then for all we can know all our individual experiences may themselves be substances.[6] But he does not, of course, endorse this view, for to do so is, again, to endorse a particular positive metaphysical position, and Hume is above all else a sceptic, someone who doesn't claim to know what the full truth is, so far as the ultimate nature of reality is concerned, although he does take us to have certain knowledge of the nature and existence of that part of reality which consists of our experiences. That said, it must be added, very firmly, that he isn't an extreme sceptic, is dismayed to be taken as one, and never questions the idea that something other than our conscious experiences does as a matter of fact exist.[7]

It may seem that verificationist positivists are obliged by their theory of meaning to say that experiences are all that exist. But this turns them into dogmatic metaphysicians. This can't be what they want. So what else can they say? They can say that experiences are all that we can *know* to exist. They can allow that it is, after all, not actually meaningless or incoherent to suppose that other things may exist, things of which we have no conception, things, perhaps, of which we can have no conception. But if they admit this in general—and they must, if we are not to dismiss them—then they must be prepared to grant that in the particular case of experiences, too, there may possibly be more to them and their existence than we know, or can know.

So they face the following choice. Either

[a] experiences are mere experiential contents, occurrences of experiential content with no hidden nature or backside or cause

—a view that risks turning into a form of radical metaphysical idealism—or

[b] experiences are not mere experiential contents, occurrences of experiential content with no hidden nature or backside or cause, and there is something more to them and their existence

—in which case some other unknown and indeed unknowable metaphysical possibility is realized.

---

[6] Our experiences are very short-lived, on his view. See also 634/App§§11–12.

[7] 'I am not such a sceptic as you may, perhaps, imagine . . .'. '*That Caesar existed, that there is such an island as Sicily*; for these propositions, I affirm, we have no demonstrative or intuitive proof. Woud you infer that I deny their truth, or even their certainty? There are many different kinds of certainty' (1754: 186).

One can accept either [a] or [b]. Either way, one is metaphysically committed. One can say that one doesn't know which of the two views is true, although one of them must be. In this case, too, one must grant that there are metaphysical matters of fact. It's an illusion (once popular) to suppose that considerations about meaning can exempt one from granting this. To think that there is some third way, some quietist *via negativa*, is intellectual dishonesty of a sort once widespread among the more extreme anti-realists of the twentieth century.

Consider three views:

[1] experiences are all that exist in reality;

[2] there may be something more than experiences, we cannot know that there is not something more, we naturally believe that there is something more, and it is certainly not entirely meaningless, or unintelligible, or incoherent, to suppose that there is something more;

[3] something other than experiences exists in reality.

Obviously Hume doesn't hold [1]. It's one of the most remarkable dogmatic metaphysical positions on record, at least as it is ordinarily understood. Does he hold [2], or [3], the negation of [1]? The answer is that he takes [3] for granted; that [3] entails [2]; and that he held [2] in any case, independently of [3].

As regards [3], and the question of the nature of physical objects, Hume says that the idea that physical objects don't have a continued existence independent of our experiences

has been peculiar to a few extravagant sceptics; who . . . maintained that opinion in words only, and were never able to bring themselves sincerely to believe it (214/1.4.2.50)

'tis in vain to ask, *Whether there be body or not?* That is a point, which we must take for granted in all our reasonings (187/1.4.2.1)

no man that reflects, ever doubted, that [experiences of the sort] we consider, when we say, *this house* and *that tree* [are] nothing but . . . fleeting copies or representations of other existences, which remain uniform and independent' of our experiences. (152/12.9)[8]

---

[8] See further the discussion of 222–3/1.4.3.9–10 in 2.5 below. Note that even the 'solipsist' view—that our sensory experiences may arise wholly from 'the creative power of the mind', or from 'the energy of the mind itself'—posits the existence of something other than one's conscious experiences.

—Objection! This can't be right. This can't be Hume's view. It follows inexorably from his theory of ideas (his theory of meaning) that we can't really get at this supposed 'something-more-than-experiences' in any way in thought or language.

This objection must be addressed to Hume himself, because it's an objection to his own words, which I've quoted. It's not correct, for Hume's theory of ideas was never put forward as a completely general theory of meaning or content. It is, rather, an account of (a way of working out) how much of the seemingly positively descriptive[9] content of any given idea or concept or expression is empirically warranted, and is therefore suitable for legitimate use in philosophy, in which, Hume holds, all concepts must be fully empirically warranted.

Hume's fundamental concern is methodological. In fact it's exactly the same as Descartes's. He wants a way of establishing the 'clear and distinct' and therefore philosophically respectable content of those concepts that are commonly employed in philosophy in the description of concrete reality.[10] He wants to do this because he holds, like Descartes, that we should never use anything other than clear and distinct concepts when doing philosophy—especially when we go so far as to make *knowledge* claims about anything.[11] As an empiricist he holds that such clear and distinct content is and can only be empirically warranted content (disagreeing directly with Descartes), and that empirically warranted content is content that is more or less literally copied from 'impressions' or sensory experiences: it's 'impression-copy-content'.[12]

---

[9] i.e. not merely referential content (a proper name like 'David' is an example of a term that has referential content but no descriptive content).

[10] Hume uses Descartes's phrase 'clear and distinct' a couple of times in the *Treatise* when discussing geometrical concepts (19/1.1.7.6, 43/1.2.4.11). He uses 'clear and distinct . . . idea' and 'clear, distinct idea' in the *Enquiry* (see 157/12.20, 164/12.28), also 'clearly and distinctly' (35/4.18); otherwise he uses 'clear' and 'distinct' separately. He also uses 'clear and precise' (52/1.3.1.7, 648/Abs§7). The fact that attention is restricted to the philosophical use of terms is almost always taken for granted—Hume is after all doing philosophy and addressing philosophers—but it's also sometimes explicit (see e.g. 648/Abs§7, 22/2.9).

[11] The restriction of the point to knowledge claims is stressed by Kant.

[12] Empiricists differ on the details of empirical warrant; Hume endorses the 'Copy Principle' according to which 'all our simple ideas in their first appearance are deriv'd from simple impressions, which are correspondent to them, and which they exactly represent' (4/1.1.1.8) or, in the *Enquiry* version, 'all our ideas or more feeble perceptions are copies of our impressions or more lively ones' (19/2.5). For a good discussion see Garrett 1997: ch. 2. The notion of a copy (*ektupon*) is in Hume's time philosophically loaded, but I'll pass over this point.

This impression-copy-content is all the clear and precise content that expressions like 'tree' or 'cause' can be allowed to have when one is doing philosophy—in so far as such expressions are taken to have positively descriptive content, rather than merely referential or existence-indicating content. And in this positive-descriptive-content sense of 'content', the term 'something-more-than-experiences' can indeed have no content at all, on Hume's terms. But this doesn't mean that we can't suppose, in a general way, when doing philosophy, that the expression 'something-more-than-experiences' can *refer*, and correspondingly, that something-more-than-experiences *exists*. And of course we can and do suppose this. Hume makes the point explicitly: 'we may well *suppose in general*' that physical objects are different from (and over and above) experiences (218/ 1.4.2.56): there's nothing illegitimate about doing this. The only problem is that it is 'impossible for us *distinctly to conceive*' this—nb. 'distinctly'.[13] This quotation comes from the *Treatise*, and Hume is equally clear in the *Enquiry*. So far as our experiences are concerned, he says, in a passage already quoted, it is a straightforward although undecidable 'question of fact' (153/12.12) whether one particular theory which postulates the existence of something more than experiences is true or false.

Some think Hume shouldn't have said this, given his theory of meaning, strictly construed. But he did say it, in many ways, and in a wholly unequivocal manner, at a crucial point in what he offered as his definitive statement of his 'philosophical . . . principles'.[14] So if it's true that he shouldn't have said it, given his theory of meaning strictly construed, the conclusion to be drawn is that he didn't construe his theory of meaning strictly in the way that many have supposed, i.e. as an exhaustive account of all the content that our concepts actually have as deployed in our thought, but rather as a claim about the meaning or content of properly empirically warranted concepts, concepts suitable for use in making clear claims in philosophy. And that is the correct conclusion.[15] Hume says that 'it seems a proposition, which will not admit of much dispute, that all our ideas are nothing but copies of our impressions, or, in

---

[13] 218/1.4.2.56. As far as I know, the importance of this point was first made clear by Wright 1983: 106–7 and Craig 1987: 123–4. See also Strawson 1989: 49–58, Kail 2007a.

[14] *Enquiry*, 'Advertisement' (1/2). For a discussion of the importance of the prefatory advertisement or warning (*avertissement*), see Strawson 2000b: §2.

[15] Here of course Hume is close to Kant. For further proof of the point, see 2.4 below.

other words, that it is impossible for us to *think* of any thing, which we have not antecedently *felt*, either by our external or internal senses' (62/7.4). But he takes this to be wholly compatible with the coherence, and indeed obvious truth, of the view that our experiences may be caused by something 'unknown' (153/12.12).[16]

One could put the point as follows. Hume's claim is not that the empirically warranted content of our ideas or concepts is all the content they actually have, although we wrongly think they have more. His claim, and his problem, is rather and precisely that they do have more content, content that we have to purge or put aside when we're trying to establish clear and distinct concepts suitable for use in philosophy. It would be wrong to think that this extra content is something that he acknowledges only unwillingly or glancingly. *Book 1 of the* Treatise *is almost wholly concerned with it.* It's concerned with the content found, for example, in our ordinary beliefs about persisting, mind-independent external objects, or in 'the idea of matter, which we fancy so clear and determinate' (232/1.4.5.1), or the idea of objective causal power. The claim is not that this content doesn't exist, or that we're mistaken in thinking that it exists.[17] The claim is that it's not properly empirically warranted or underwritten or justified or 'intelligible', hence not passed for use in philosophy when it comes to making knowledge claims or reaching justified conclusions. It is, on the contrary, and in Hume's own many and varied words, indistinct rather than distinct; confused and obscure rather than clear; imperfect, deficient, inexact, relative, inaccurate, unfixed, inadequate, imprecise, loose, uncertain, indeterminate, obscure, implicit, distant, vulgar, 'fiction'-involving, and so on.[18] It's plain

---

[16] In effect , 'think of' is, short for 'think clearly and precisely of'. The passage continues 'I have endeavoured . . . to explain and prove this proposition, and have expressed my hopes, that, by a proper application of it, men may reach a greater clearness and precision in philosophical reasonings, than what they have hitherto been able to attain (62/7.4).

[17] Some of his remarks can be read in this way if taken literally, but only by superficial readers. Here we should call upon Kant's exegetical wisdom in the closing paragraph of his Preface to the second edition of the *Critique of Pure Reason* (a remark presumably motivated by reactions to the first edition): 'if we take single passages, torn from their context, and compare them with one another, contradictions are not likely to be lacking, especially in a work that is written with any freedom of expression . . . ; but they are easily resolved by those who have mastered the idea of the whole' (1787: Bxliv).

[18] Indistinct, see e.g. 162/1.3.14.14, 218/1.4.2.56, 22/2.9; confused, obscure, unclear, see e.g. 33/1.2.3.1, 162/1.3.14.14, 648/Abs§7, 78n/7.29n; imperfect, see e.g. 18–23/1.1.7.2–14, 222/1.4.3.8, 77/7.29; deficient, see e.g. 267/1.4.7.6; inexact, see e.g. 45/1.2.4.17; merely 'relative', see e.g. 62/1.2.6.9; inaccurate, see e.g. 53/1.2.4.33; unfixed, see e.g. 189/1.4.2.6; inadequate, see e.g.

that neither an idea nor its content can have any of these properties if it doesn't exist.[19]

Suppose we introduce the neutral term 'mental element' as a general name for any putative idea or mental content. Sometimes Hume uses the word 'idea' in a normative way, given which only mental elements that are clear and distinct qualify as ideas at all (234/1.4.5.6, 658/Abs§28). This has misled some commentators into thinking that this is his general position (see further 2.4 below), although he uses the word 'idea' far more often in a wider, non-normative way to talk as much of mental elements that are not empirically respectable as of those that are. Taken in this wider sense, an idea is any mental element, fictional or not, clear and precise or not, which functions in our thinking in the same general sort of way as mental elements that are empirically legitimate ideas do.

Hume, then, is clear on the point that one can't form any conception of a concretely existing *something-that-is-something-more-than-experiences* that is both philosophically legitimate and genuinely descriptively contentful, on the terms of his empiricist theory of clear and distinct meaning.[20] But this doesn't prevent him from allowing that we can legitimately suppose that this something-more-than-experiences exists, and taking it for granted that it does.

If one adopts any sort of strongly empiricist approach, one will presumably hold that even the entirely unspecific idea or concept of *something* is derived from experience in some way. So be it. It will none the less remain what it is: an idea whose whole semantic point is to be entirely unspecific, to assert existence while having, precisely, no positively descriptive

---

160/1.3.14.10; imprecise, see e.g. 50/1.2.4.27, 67n/7.15n; loose, see e.g. 49/1.2.4.25, 33n/4.16n, 77n/7.29n; uncertain, see e.g. 78n/7.29n; indeterminate, see e.g. 50/1.2.4.29, 162/1.3.14.1; obscure (notion), see e.g. 37/1.2.4.24; implicit (notion), see e.g. 48/1.2.4.24; distant (notion), see e.g. 49/1.2.4.25; vulgar, see e.g. 67n/7.15n; 'fiction'-involving, see passim. Note that a fiction-involving idea is not necessarily incorrect, on Hume's view, it's just empirically unwarranted; see Strawson 1989: 55n. 36.

[19] I've left 'incomprehensible' and 'unintelligible' out of this catalogue, although mental elements may also be perfectly 'incomprehensible' and 'unintelligible', on Hume's terms. See further 2.4 below.

[20] Unless something like the Lockean resemblance claim can be made out—see n. 4 and the reference there. In the end Hume leaves this question unsettled; the key point for him is that even if it could be made out we couldn't know this.

content of any sort. All that Hume has to allow, in order to say that the idea of something-more-than-experiences does have respectable content, on the terms of his theory of meaning, and isn't contradictory in so far as it does have content, is that the entirely unspecific idea of something, or equivalently of something-that-exists, doesn't itself inevitably refer to experiences and only to experiences, given its source.

Does he allow this? Of course. No thoughtful sceptic can do otherwise. No sensible empiricist can do otherwise. No sane philosopher can do otherwise. We can in Hume's terminology 'suppose' that there may exist something of which we have and can have no empirically legitimate, empirically contentful, 'conception'. It may be said that the polemical young Hume of the *Treatise*, following the radical empiricist thought to its intoxicating root, was tempted by the fantastic anti-realist view that even the entirely unspecific idea of *something* can only ever refer to experiences, given its aetiology. A thousand passages show that this is not his view. In the *Treatise* he declares that he will 'go upon the supposition' that 'there is both an external and internal world' (218/1.4.2.57), the supposition that there are objects or bodies that are not experiences; for ''tis in vain to ask, *Whether there be body or not?* That is a point, which we must take for granted in all our reasonings' (187/1.4.2.1). In the *Enquiry* he is admirably blunt, in a passage that bears considerable repetition: 'It is', he says, 'a question of fact, whether the experiences of the senses be produced by external objects ... entirely different from them, though resembling them' (153/12.12). It's undecidable, certainly, but it is for all that a straightforward question of fact.[21]

I've already quoted Hume's remark in the *Enquiry* that 'no man that reflects, ever doubted, that [experiences of the sort] we consider, when we say, *this house* and *that tree*', are 'nothing but ... fleeting copies or representations of other existences, which remain uniform and independent' of our perceptions (152/12.9). It's worth quoting again, for he himself is a man who reflects, hence a man who never doubts that the things we're talking about, when we talk about physical objects, are not just experiences. More important for present purposes, though, is the fact that this passage refutes

---

[21] What about the claim he makes when discussing the nature of belief in the Appendix to the *Treatise*: 'we have no abstract idea of existence, distinguishable and separable from the idea of particular objects' (623/App§2)? This quotation, taken in context, doesn't support the extreme anti-realist view. Nor does Hume's account of the impossibility of conceiving a specific difference between an object and a perception (241/1.4.5.19). See further 2.4 below.

the idea that Hume thinks that it's *unintelligible* (in the modern philosophical sense of the word 'unintelligible', given which it is used to mean 'incoherent') to suppose that physical objects are anything more than our experiences or perceptions. Moving back to the *Treatise*, Hume says that 'the perceptions of the mind are perfectly known', whereas 'the essence and composition of external bodies are . . . obscure' (366/2.2.6.2). Nothing can be both perfectly known and obscure.

Consider briefly, by way of further illustration, how this argument runs in the case of causation. Hume either holds that

(C1) regular succession[22] is all there is to causation, in reality

or that

(C2) there may be something more than regular succession, we can't know that there isn't something more, we naturally believe that there is something more, and it's certainly not entirely meaningless or unintelligible or incoherent to suppose that there is something more

or something stronger than (C2), i.e. the negation of (C1), i.e. that

(C3) something more than regular succession exists in reality, so far as the phenomenon of causation is concerned.

On the terms of his official theory of meaning, Hume thinks that when we consider the nature of causation in so far as it is or may be something more than regular succession, we can't satisfactorily get at or comprehend the 'something more' in thought or language, because we can't form any idea of it that has content that is both positively descriptively contentful and empirically legitimate. We can certainly suppose that the something more exists, however, and Hume takes it for granted that it does. He is merely concerned to stress the point that we can't know its nature—in opposition to the majority of his contemporaries, who were convinced that we could.[23] In one rather beautiful sentence Hume remarks that

the scenes of the universe are continually shifting, and one object follows another in an uninterrupted succession; but the power or force, which actuates the whole

---

[22] I'm understanding the notion of regular succession in Hume's way as a matter of spatio-temporal priority and contiguity between particulars and constant conjunction (in respect of spatiotemporal contiguity) between types of particulars. (For a reservation about spatial contiguity, see 3.7 below.)

[23] Most of them—including the older Newton—thought that causal power had to involve mental volition of some sort.

machine, is entirely concealed from us, and never discovers itself in any of the sensible qualities of body (63–4/7.8)

and here his view seems very clear indeed. 'The power or force which [actually] actuates the whole machine . . . of the universe' certainly exists, but its nature is entirely concealed from us in so far as it is something more than or other than regular succession.[24]

The point is hardly less clear in the *Treatise*, when he's arguing that we have no idea of the nature of necessity or causal power or force as it is in the objects: 'I am, indeed', he says,

ready to allow, that there may be several qualities both in material and immaterial objects, with which we are utterly unacquainted; and if we please to call these *power* or *efficacy*, 'twill be of little consequence to the world. But when, *instead of meaning these unknown qualities*, we make the terms of power and efficacy *signify something, of which we have a clear idea* . . . , obscurity and error *begin then* to take place, and we are led astray by a false philosophy. (168/1.3.14.27)

This is because the only clear idea of necessity we have is derived from the felt quality of an internal 'impression of reflexion', a mental feeling of determination, and is therefore 'incompatible with those objects, to which we apply it' when we try to suppose that it is to be found in the world (168/1.3.14.27). We can and do use 'power' or 'efficacy' to 'mean' (designate, refer to) these unknown qualities, but this is useless when we come to do philosophy, for we're in the dark, so far as the nature of these unknown qualities is concerned. As soon as we try to use these words with *clear meaning*, as philosophy demands that we do, they can no longer possibly mean or apply to what we're using them to mean or apply to, because their only clear meaning derives from an inner mental experience, a 'feeling of determination'.

More generally now, consider the suggestion that there may be aspects of reality that are completely unintelligible to us in the ordinary sense of the word, i.e. un-understandable by us or incomprehensible to us. Bare common sense—not to mention a minimum degree of modesty or sceptical reserve—requires us to grant this. But some seem to think that Hume the sceptic is denying it. This is because they think he's using the word 'unintelligible' in the strong modern philosophical sense, according to which to say that something x is unintelligible is to say that the idea of

---

[24] I've argued this point in a number of places (see e.g. Strawson 1989, 2000b).

x is in fact incoherent, and hence that x can't possibly exist. On this view, to the extent that Hume says or implies that the existence of anything other than experiences is unintelligible, he's committed to the view that only experiences exist and can exist.

But Hume doesn't mean this by the word 'unintelligible'. He doesn't use it to mean or imply 'incoherent' in this sense. He uses it in the natural and literal way that is standard outside philosophy—as when we say that a message is unintelligible, meaning simply that we can't understand it, although it exists. If he had used 'unintelligible' to mean 'incoherent' in the way that is now standard in philosophy, he would have had to have been a dogmatic metaphysician after all, someone who held as a matter of certainty that only experiences exist and can exist. What's more, he would have reached this full-blown ontological conclusion—that only experiences exist—first by arguing that experiences are all we can know, and secondly by arguing that they're all that we can think (about) or mean. On this view, Hume takes it that absolute metaphysical certainty about the ultimate nature of reality isn't difficult to achieve. It's not a matter of 'sophistry and illusion' after all. In fact it's really easy. It can be done without vacating one's armchair.

1.2 The [E]–[S]–[O] move

Many commentators have supposed that the fundamental move in Hume's philosophy is from an epistemological claim of the form

[E] y is/are all we can *know* of x

to a corresponding semantic claim of the form

[S] y is/are all we can *mean*—all we can manage to mean—by the idea or concept (term) x

to a full-on ontological or metaphysical conclusion of the form

[O] y is/are all that x *is* (all that xs *are*).[25]

---

[25] See Strawson 1989: ch. 3. It's arguable that the popularity of this move is the key to nearly everything that went wrong in philosophy from Locke until the end of the twentieth century. Compare Carnap 1950.

The move is meant to underlie—indeed constitute—his account of external objects, the mind, and causation. If one replaces 'x' by 'external objects', one replaces 'y' by 'experiences with certain sorts of resemblance, constancy, and coherence characteristics' (for the details, see 1.4.2 of the *Treatise*). If one replaces 'x' by 'the self' or 'the mind', one can replace 'y' simply by 'experiences' (for the details, see 1.4.6 of the *Treatise*). If one replaces 'x' by 'causation', one replaces 'y' by 'regular succession' or 'constant conjunction' and/or 'feeling of determination' (for the details, see 1.3.14 of the *Treatise*).

As far as objects and the mind are concerned, then, we have

[E] experiences of a certain kind are all we can *know* of x,

so

[S] experiences of a certain kind are all we can *mean* by the idea or concept (term) x,

so

[O] all x *is* (all xs *are*) is (are) experiences of a certain kind.

[O] follows from [S], because when the idea (term) *x* occurs in our thought, then, given [S], it inevitably just means: experiences of a certain kind. So [O] is true: x just is/are experiences of a certain kind. For *x* just means or is an idea of experiences of a certain kind, and experiences of a certain kind are, tautologically, experiences of that kind. In this scheme, Hume's theory of ideas or meaning is taken to be a completely general account of mental content rather than what it actually is, i.e. an account of empirically warranted, philosophically respectable content. According to the theory of ideas or meaning so construed, all ideas or concepts derive all their content from the content of experiences by the copying process already referred to.

The view that Hume makes the [E]–[S]–[O] move in this form was widespread during the twentieth century, although it turns him (once again) from a sceptic into a dogmatic metaphysician who claims certainty about the ultimate nature of things, and who claims, in particular, to know that experiences are all that exist. This is rather hard on Hume, for he says himself that ignorance, even necessary ignorance, isn't a good reason for denying the possible existence of anything (72–3/7.25). Even Berkeley allows that it's 'absurd for any man to argue against the existence of [a] thing, from his having no direct and positive notion of it'. It's only where 'we have not even a relative notion of it', Berkeley says in his *Third Dialogue*, that we 'employ words to no manner of purpose, without any design or signification whatever'; 'many things', he says, 'for anything I know, may exist, whereof neither I nor any other man has or can have any idea or notion whatsoever' (1713: 177, 184). Hume agrees. In a passage which I've already used as an epigraph, and which will be a constant refrain, he says that 'the essence of the mind' is 'unknown to us with that of external bodies'.[26] Indeed; but—and therefore—it exists.

Locke makes a similar move. He holds that the 'real essence' of gold is completely unknown to us, and his theory of ideas, like Hume's and Berkeley's, obliges him to conclude that in so far as the word 'gold' carries a 'tacit reference to the real essence' of gold, as it clearly does in common use, it has '*no signification at all*'; it is in other words 'meaningless', 'being put for somewhat, whereof we have no idea at all' (*Essay* 3.10.19). And yet it does succeed in referring, and certainly has meaning in that sense—as Locke allows.

Kant makes a similar move in similar language. He says, on the one hand, that the categories, which include the concept of cause, 'have only an empirical use, and have *no meaning whatever* when not applied to objects of possible experience'. On the other hand, he says that 'in *thinking*', and *a fortiori* in intelligible—hence contentful, hence meaningful—thinking, 'the categories are not limited by the conditions of our sensible intuition, but have an unlimited field. It is only *knowledge* of what we think . . . that requires intuition'. He allows, in other words, and in the particular case of causation, that there may be causation that is not spatio-temporal. He allows that it's intelligible to suppose that this is so, and at one point offers a highly general characterization of causation—it's the 'because something is, something else must be' relation (1781/7: B288)—that doesn't limit its application to spatio-temporal phenomena as given in sensibility. He claims only, and fully consistently, given his overall framework, that we could not, when applying the concept of causation beyond the bounds of sense (sensibility), make any claims to knowledge.[27]

---

[26] xvii/Int§8; I'll regularly omit the reference.

[27] See B166n; see also B309, A696/B724 and *passim*. Kant is independently committed to the existence of non-spatio-temporal causation by his moral philosophy, and discusses Hume's views on causation with specific reference to this point in his *Critique of Practical Reason* (1788).

The general point—that one can intelligibly suppose something to exist and be available for valid or meaningful reference even though one has no positively contentful conception of its nature—was routine in Hume's time, as it is now. So too is the idea that one can have reason to suppose that some such thing exists. Hume continually stresses the fact that there may be aspects of reality of which we can form no legitimate positively descriptively contentful conception on the terms of his theory of empirically warranted meaning—aspects of reality that are in that sense wholly unintelligible to us. This is an integral part of his scepticism, quite apart from being an integral part of any sound philosophy. Only certain radical empiricist, anti-realist, verificationist philosophers of the twentieth century were able to go so far as to deny that meaning in the sense of reference could be intelligibly supposed to extend beyond experience.

1.3 The [E]–[S]–[O] move and physical objects

In the case of physical objects, the [E]–[S]–[O] move goes like this:

(E) All we can ever know or observe of physical objects are perceptions or experiences,

i.e. mental goings-on considered just as such. So

(S) all we can ever legitimately manage to mean by ideas or concepts (terms) like *physical object* or *table* or *chair* are experiences (actual or possible).

So

(O) all that physical objects actually are, are experiences.

So phenomenalism is true. Not just mild methodological phenomenalism, but mad metaphysical phenomenalism, the view that physical objects are definitely nothing more than experiences. Or, in other terms, the view that statements about physical objects reduce without any loss of semantic or ontological import to statements about experiences. On this view, even if something other than experiences exists, we can't 'manage to mean' this something. Except that even this way of putting it won't do. For on this view the sentence 'On this view, even if something other than experiences exists, we can't "manage to mean" this something' is already illegitimate. It's illegitimate because the clause 'if something other than experiences exists' can't really contain the reference to something other than experiences that it purports to contain.

This is not Hume's view. For one thing, he holds both that the 'the essence of the mind' is 'unknown to us' (xvii/Int§8), and that 'the perceptions of the mind are perfectly known' (366/2.2.6.2). Putting aside the point that this proves that he doesn't think that experiences are all there is to the mind (see Part 2), the present point is that it proves that he doesn't think that we can't 'refer beyond experiences', however 'unintelligible' or 'incomprehensible' such references are so far as they purport to involve positively descriptive content. Again: it is 'a question of fact, whether the perceptions of the senses be produced by external objects...entirely different from them' (153/12.12). Here he means external objects that are not themselves experiences, but are 'entirely different from' experiences, and 'produce' experiences. Remember the *Treatise*: 'we may well suppose in general' that physical objects are different from experiences; there is no problem with this. The problem is that it is 'impossible for us *distinctly* to conceive' of this (218/1.4.2.56).

Hume said things in the *Treatise* that invite the interpretation I'm rejecting (if only from careless readers). He was, when he wrote that great book, lit up by what he later called the 'ardor of youth', and the intense and dubious pleasures of philosophical iconoclasm. For all that, the idea that things may exist of which we neither have nor can have any impression-based idea or conception is part of the basic framework of the book. It's strongly stressed in the introduction, and Hume makes it explicit in a number of different ways.[28] I've already drawn attention to passages in which he distinguishes between what we can suppose and what we can conceive.[29] A genuine *conception* of something must have impression-based descriptively contentful (not merely referential) content. A *supposition*, by contrast, can be genuinely about something even if it lacks any such impression-based content, and is therefore a merely 'relative' idea.

Suppose you go to your room and find a peculiar mess. You have absolutely no idea what caused it, but you suppose, reasonably, that something did. Call this something 'x'. Clearly you can refer to and

---

[28] He's particularly concerned to stress it after Book 1 of the *Treatise* has been published, in one of the Appendix passages which he designated to be inserted in the main text (638–9/1.2.5.56).

[29] Cf. e.g. 67–8/1.2.6.8–9, 218/1.4.2.56, 241–2/1.4.5.20, 151–3/12.8–12.

think about x simply as 'whatever caused this mess'. Here you have a merely relative idea of x. More generally, consider your experiences of tables, chairs, and so on. As a philosophical sceptic, let us say, you have no idea what gives rise to them or produces them, but you naturally suppose that something—call it 'x'—does, and you may very well be right (of course you are). Clearly, again, you can refer to and think about x simply as 'whatever causes these experiences'. Here you have a merely relative idea of x. You have no positive idea of its nature, no impression-based conception of it. You can't even be absolutely certain that it exists. You know of it only indirectly, by its supposed relation to something you do have direct experience of—your experiences. Here you 'suppose an external universe' (151/12.7), as we all do, without claiming to have any certain knowledge of its nature. The point is an old one.

Some think that little weight can be placed on the fact that Hume makes a distinction between what we can suppose and what we can conceive, because Hume himself doesn't make much of it.[30] This, how-ever, is both false and a *non sequitur*. It could be granted, for present purposes, that Hume doesn't make much of the distinction, although he makes as much of it as he needs, and relies on it constantly (to see this, search 'suppos' in an electronic copy of his texts). It could even be granted that Hume, in the high heat of his youth, sees the necessity of making the distinction between what we can suppose and what we can conceive as somewhat annoying. The fact remains that it's something he finds himself obliged to record explicitly, in the course of his sceptical progress. He duly does so, and he does so clearly and unambiguously.[31] He handles the issue just as he should. He advances to the edge of the wild anti-realist thesis, the thesis that leads to mad metaphysical phenomenalism, in accordance with the unrestrained empiricist theory of meaning. Then he draws back in just the right way, acknowledging that it is at least intelligible to suppose that unintelligible things—things other than experiences—exist, as in the passage quoted on page 12:

---

[30]   Cf. e.g. Blackburn 1993. For criticism of Blackburn, see Strawson 2000b: §6.

[31]   Recall that he is, when arguing that we can have no idea of causation in objects, 'indeed, ready to allow, that there may be several qualities both in material and in immaterial objects, with which we are utterly unacquainted' (168/1.3.14.27). Here too he is clear that the realm of existence does not cease where the realm of words or positively contentful conceptions ceases.

I am, indeed, ready to allow, that there may be several qualities both in material and immaterial objects, with which we are utterly unacquainted; and if we please to call these **power** or **efficacy**, 'twill be of little consequence to the world. But when, instead of meaning these unknown qualities, we make the terms of power and efficacy *signify something, of which we have a clear idea* . . . obscurity and error begin then to take place, and we are led astray by a false philosophy (168/1.3.14.27).

We can certainly 'mean' these unknown qualities in the sense of referring to them. We can operate, as we do, with a vague and unwarranted notion of power or efficacy in talking of the 'connexion' we don't understand.[32] What we can't do is suppose that the only empirically legitimate idea of necessity we have can apply to these unknown qualities, or constitute any kind of conception of objective necessity; for the empirically legitimate idea of necessity is derived from a wholly subjective experience of determination in the mind.

The acknowledgement that it's intelligible to suppose that things other than experiences exist is, then, a necessary part of Hume's philosophy; for reasons already given. He has to grant that thought and language can reach beyond experiences in such a way that the thought that something other than experiences exists can be allowed to be intelligible and possibly true. If he doesn't, then he is (once again) condemned to dogmatic metaphysics. He's committed to the view that the statement 'All that exist are experiences' is *provably true*. He's landed with a form of metaphysical certainty that he can't possibly tolerate, as a sceptic who correctly denies the possibility of attaining final knowledge about the ultimate nature of (non-mental) reality.

This Hume is an extravagant fanatic of the sort he dismissed, someone who thinks metaphysical certainty is cheap—someone who thinks that one can infer necessary non-existence from (inevitable, necessary) ignorance. Only a fool would do such a thing, and Hume explicitly denies the validity of this inference in his reply to the Cartesian Occasionalists in the *Enquiry*. The Occasionalists, he remarks, think that we have to attribute all power to God because we're ignorant of the nature of causal power in the world—'totally ignorant of the power on which depends the mutual operation of bodies', and 'no less ignorant of that power on which depends the operation of mind on body, or of body on mind' (70/7.21). Hume

---

[32] 'Connexion' is Hume's preferred neutral word for talking of causation thought of as something whose nature we can't understand.

fully agrees with them about the extent of our ignorance, but he then points out that our ignorance doesn't stop there. For we are, he observes, equally ignorant of the 'manner or force by which . . . even the supreme mind, operates either on itself or on body'. And then he makes the obvious move:

> Were our ignorance, therefore, a good reason for rejecting anything, we should be led into that principle of denying all energy in the Supreme Being as much as in the grossest matter. (72–3/7.25)

Here he states a basic principle of scepticism, annihilating the Occasion-alists' argument in passing. Ignorance—even necessary ignorance—isn't a good reason for denying the possible existence of anything. As Hume knows—as any sane philosopher must allow—it makes sense to suppose (and is doubtless true) that there are things that are incomprehensible and unknowable by us. One can't infer non-existence from ignorance. One can't infer non-existence from unintelligibility (incomprehensibility, un-understandability). Like Kant, like any reasonable philosopher, Hume grants that we can make suppositions about existence that extend beyond the bounds of sense even though we can't attain any certain knowledge of what (if anything) lies beyond the bounds of sense. He grants this even though he's faced with a considerable problem about the exact nature or content of such suppositions, given his meaning-empiricism, which ob-liges him to say that there is something seriously problematic, incomplete, or misleading—defective, inaccurate, imperfect, loose, confused, 'fiction'-involving, etc.—about the content of any such suppositions.[33]

In its extreme form, meaning-empiricism is obliged to say that these thoughts have no content at all, in so far as they purport to be about something other than what is immediately given in the content of experi-ence. But this, of course, and again, is not Hume's view. He takes it for granted that there exists something other than experiences and, *a fortiori*, that it makes sense to suppose that this is so. His scepticism and his deep philosophical common sense combine to fix him in this view. Just as real realism entails scepticism, so real scepticism entails at least this amount of

---

[33] As already remarked, they couldn't have any of these defects if they didn't have any content. Hume is sometimes struck by the thought that attempts to reach beyond experi-ences, e.g. in expressing the supposition that there are external objects, must somehow still use impression-based contents, given the terms of his theory of ideas. Cf. e.g. 218, lines 6–11/1.4.2.56, 241; and lines 20–4/1.4.5.19.

speculative realism. This he knows.[34] It is, once again, 'a question of fact, whether the perceptions of the senses be produced by external objects, resembling them' (153/12.12), although it is a question we can never answer.

Hume, then, doesn't make the [E]–[S]–[O] move. But all one needs to do, in order to represent his thought correctly, is make a small adjustment to [S]—an adjustment which crucially changes the status of [O]. The corrected version of [S] can be variously expressed, for example as follows:

[S] y is all we can mean by the idea or concept (term) *x* so far as *x* has any *empirically warranted positive descriptive* content, and therefore has a fully legitimate use in philosophy

and the conclusion that [S] permits, given this adjustment, is no longer [O], an outright ontological conclusion, but [OE], a qualified, ontological-epistemological conclusion:

[OE] y is all that x is or involves *so far as we have any empirically warranted positively descriptively contentful conception of* x

i.e. a conception of x of a sort that we can legitimately deploy in doing philosophy, a discipline which aims at certain knowledge. This is Hume's position, the position of a consistent, moderate sceptic.

1.4 Hume's definitions of cause

In the case of causation, considered as an objective property of reality, the [E]–[S]–[O] move goes like this:

(E) all we can ever know or observe of causation is regular succession,

so

(S) all we can legitimately manage to mean by the idea or concept (term) *causation* is regular succession,

so

(O) all that causation actually is, is regular succession.

The moderation of [O] from an ontological claim to an ontological-epistemological claim, following the adjustment of [S] to read, say,

[S] all we can legitimately, positively descriptively manage to mean by the idea or concept (term) *causation*, when doing philosophy, and therefore using only properly empirically warranted ideas (terms), is regular succession

gives us Hume's actual view:

[OE] regular succession is all that causation is or involves so far as we have any empirically warranted positively contentful conception of its nature.

There are many points at which Hume uses qualifying phrases of exactly this sort. His primary point is epistemological, not ontological.[35]

The point can be reaffirmed by considering Hume's two definitions of cause. It's clear who he's targeting in this part of his discussion: all those of his contemporaries who think that they know more about causation than it is in fact possible to know—all those who think that they have some sort of genuine understanding of its ultimate or intrinsic nature. Hume wants to show them that they're wrong. He wants to prove that we're entirely ignorant of the nature of causation in so far as it involves something more than regular succession. This ignorance is what has to be shown and argued for from all sides, in Hume's view. It has to be argued for because it is initially very hard to believe, very surprising, for philosophers and ordinary people alike. Why is this? Because, he says, 'our thoughts and enquiries are ... every moment, employed about' the relation of cause and effect (76/7.29). Our practical thoughts, as we negotiate the world, are saturated with causal assumptions, expectations, predictions, speculations, and so on. It is accordingly extremely startling—a 'violent ... paradox' (166/1.3.14.24)—to be told that one has absolutely no grasp of the intrinsic nature of this phenomenon.

Hume begins by saying that 'the ideas which we form concerning' cause are

so imperfect ... , that it is impossible to give any just definition of cause, except what is drawn from something extraneous and foreign to it. (76/7.29)

Here he's referring to the two definitions that immediately follow, which specify the philosophically legitimate content that the idea of cause has given its impression sources. They tell us what we can legitimately manage

---

[35] See in particular Craig 1987: ch. 2, Strawson 1989: 10–12. Here I'm putting aside Hume's account of how our experience of a mental 'feeling of determination' contributes to our idea of causation (see e.g. 165/1.3.14.20).

to mean, on the terms of the theory of ideas, when we talk about causes. The first defines causation as constant conjunction or regular succession, the second defines it in terms of a feeling of determination in the mind (76–7/7.29, 170/1.3.14.31, 172/1.3.14.35). Both are held to be imperfect because they can't representationally encompass causation or power 'as it is in itself' (77 n/7.29 n.). They can define it only by reference to something other than itself.

An enormous amount has been written about the content of the two definitions. My concern here is only with Hume's view of what they achieve—his view that it is actually impossible for us to give anything other than an 'imperfect' definition of cause. Some deny that Hume thinks his definitions are imperfect, because he says in the *Treatise* that they're 'exact' and 'precise' and 'just', or as just as any definitions of cause can be (169/1.3.14.30, 170/1.3.14.31; compare *Enquiry* 76/7.29). This, however, is a *non sequitur*, and obscures the crucial point, which is precisely that Hume holds that the definitions are imperfect *in spite of* the fact that he thinks they're exact, precise, and just.[36]

What can he mean by 'imperfect'? He's very clear about what he means. He means that the definitions don't really capture the true nature of causation at all. The trouble is that

we cannot remedy this inconvenience, or attain any more perfect definition, which may point out *that circumstance in the cause, which gives it a connexion with its effect.* (77/7.29)

The trouble, in other words, is that although there is something about the cause-event in virtue of which it's connected with its effect, in any particular case, we can't form any genuine descriptively contentful conception of this something on the terms of the theory of ideas.

This quotation suffices to refute the view that Hume held a regularity theory of causation, for if causation in the objects were just regular succession or constant conjunction, there would be no inconvenience or imperfection in the first definition at all, and in giving the first definition, we could hardly be said to be in the position of finding it 'impossible to give any just definition of cause, except what is drawn from something extraneous and foreign to it'.[37]

---

[36] The words 'exact' and 'precise' disappear from the corresponding passage in the *Enquiry*.

[37] For an attempt to reply to this point, see Millican 2009.

That's a refutation (for another, see pp. 110–11 below). But some may say that all that Hume means, when he says that one has to refer to circumstances foreign to the cause, is that one has to go beyond the individual cause-event considered on its own: one has to mention the effect-event, and other events of the same type as the cause-event and effect-event, and even the human mind. So let us suppose that this is part of what he meant.[38] The present point retains its full force. For Hume says that the definitions are imperfect specifically because they can't 'point out that circumstance in the cause, which [actually] gives it a connexion with its effect' (77/7.29; compare 67–8/7.17). That is, there's something about the cause itself which the definitions can't capture or represent: in fact they leave out the essential thing. The imperfection in question is the imperfection that definitions have when they don't fully capture the nature of the thing that they're meant to be definitions of. We can't give a perfect definition of cause because of our ignorance of its nature. All we can encompass in our definition are its observable manifestations—its regular-succession manifestations (first definition), and the feelings of necessity or determination or habits of inference in the mind to which these give rise (second definition).

There has been a lot of speculation about the differences between Hume's use of the word 'definition' and our present-day use. Edmund Burke's remarks about definition—made in 1757, nine years after the publication of the first edition of the first *Enquiry*, in a work which Hume read—are illuminating.[39] 'When we define', Burke writes,

we seem in danger of circumscribing nature within the bounds of our own notions, which we often . . . form out of a limited and partial consideration of the object before us, instead of extending our ideas to take in all that nature comprehends, according to her manner of combining . . . .

A definition may be very exact, and yet go but a very little way towards informing us of the nature of the thing defined. (1757: 12)

Here, I propose, Burke uses 'definition' and 'exact' in exactly the same way as Hume. So too Priestley in 1778:

---

[38] Cf. Wright 2000. In Strawson 1989: chs. 14–15, which focus on Hume's discussion of causation in the *Treatise*, I try to marshal the strongest prima facie evidence for the view of Hume that I reject here.

[39] He called it 'a very pretty treatise' in a letter to Adam Smith (1759: 51), telling Smith he had sent Burke a copy of Smith's *Theory of Moral Sentiments* (he certainly wasn't being ironic, as has been suggested).

A definition of any particular thing . . . cannot be anything more than an enumeration of its known properties. (1778: 40)

A definition of a natural phenomenon, as opposed to a definition of a geometrical figure, records human understanding's best take on that phenomenon. As such, it may be very 'exact', 'precise', and 'just' while also being very 'imperfect', 'limited and partial' in its representation of the nature of the phenomenon defined.[40]

Hume restates his position as follows:

If we examine the operations of body, and the productions of effects from their causes, we shall find that all our faculties can never carry us farther in our knowledge of [the] relation [of cause and effect] than *barely* to observe that particular objects are **constantly conjoin'd** together [cf. the first definition], and that the mind is carried, by a **customary transition**, from the appearance of one to the belief of the other [cf. the second definition]. (92/8.21)

That is, all we can get to know of causation is the content of the two imperfect definitions. That is, we can't get very far. We can 'barely' (merely) observe this much. So these two definitions don't say what causation actually is; they just express all we know of it. And

this conclusion concerning human ignorance [is] the result of the strictest scrutiny of this subject. . . . [W]e know nothing farther of causation . . . than *merely* the **constant conjunction** of objects, and the consequent *inference* of the mind from one to another. (92/8.21)

The conclusion is a conclusion about human ignorance. There's more to causation, but we're ignorant of it. Newton, Hume's great model, takes exactly the same line in his *Principia*.[41] The trouble is that 'the powers, by which bodies operate, are entirely unknown' to us (652/Abs§15). They are in that respect exactly on a par with 'the essence of the mind', which is 'equally unknown to us with that of external bodies'.

---

[40] This use of 'definition' is not restricted to the eighteenth century. Russell uses the word in the same way when discussing the nature of matter: 'all that we ought to assume is series of groups of events, connected by discoverable laws. These series we may *define* as "matter". Whether there *is* matter in any other sense, no one can tell' (1927: 93). Russell makes it clear that to give a definition is not to make an ontological declaration. Compare Eddington's remark that 'we know nothing about the intrinsic nature of space, and so it is quite easy to conceive it satisfactorily' (1928: 51). It's in this sense that Hume's definitions of cause are exact and satisfactory.

[41] Cf. e.g. *Principia* Definition 8. The parallel is discussed in Strawson 1989: 202–3. For further discussion of the status of the two definitions, see especially Craig 1987: 102–9.

The situation, to quote now only from the *Treatise*, is that

we have no other *notion* of cause and effect, but that of certain objects, which have been always conjoin'd together, and which in all past instances have been found inseparable. *We cannot penetrate into the reason of the conjunction* (93/1.3.6.15)

just as we can't penetrate into the essence of the mind, or of external bodies. As to the objective facts of causation or 'real connexion betwixt causes and effects',[42]

two objects are connected by the relation of cause and effect, when the one produces a motion or any action in the other (12/1.1.4.5).

But we can't observe this real connection. In fact—to quote, finally, a passage which is particularly revealing, but which requires care, in the context of the last two quotations, because it is one of the places in which Hume uses the expression 'the relation of cause and effect' to refer to cause and effect in so far as it is something of which we have a positively contentful conception—

the only conclusion we can draw from the existence of one thing to that of another, is by means of [1] the relation of cause and effect, which *shews*, that there is [2] a connexion betwixt them, and that *the existence of one is dependent on that of the other.* [3] The idea of this relation is deriv'd from past experience [of constant conjunction] ... (212/1.4.2.46)

In this passage we have three distinct things. There is, first, [3], the legitimate *idea* of the relation of cause and effect which we derive from experience of constant conjunction. Then there is [1], the relation of cause and effect itself, considered as something of which we have a legitimate positively contentful conception in having [3], as something we can detect in things, something which can thereby 'shew' us something and of which we can therefore make use in drawing con-clusions (the relation of cause and effect as defined in the first definition of cause). Finally, there is [2], the relation of causation itself as it is unknowably in the objects. And what is of particular interest and importance in this quotation is the distinction between [1] and [2]: [1], the relation of cause and effect in the sense of something which we

[42] 168/1.3.14.27. 'By "real connexion" used as a technical term, Hume means (at least) a connection between two objects that is more than simply an associative relation in the imagination' (Garrett 1997: 181).

can detect, and which can thereby 'shew' us something, is explicitly distinguished from [2], i.e. the actual causal connection, the relation of *real existential dependence* between objects.[43] Hume's claim is that if [1] is detected as holding between two (types of) objects A and B, then that *shows* that something *other* than [1], i.e. [2], is present. When the conditions laid down in the constant-conjunction or regularity-theory definition of cause look to be fulfilled by A and B, we can conclude from that that there is a real causal connection between them, a relation of existential dependence (whose intrinsic nature we can't know). Observed constant conjunction is *evidence* for existential dependence, i.e. real causal connection. But 'we cannot penetrate into the reason of the conjunction'.[44] I'll return to this issue in 2.7.

1.5 Hume's Philo

Hume was a sceptic. As a consistent sceptic, he wouldn't have claimed to know for certain that there was causal power or objective necessity in the universe if he had been asked, although he had no doubt about the matter—no doubt that there was something in 'the cause, which gives it a connexion with its effect' (77/7.29). He did, furthermore, as a sceptic, and in the wake of Berkeley, consider—and reject—the metaphysical possibility that there might be no genuinely external physical objects. That said, there's no evidence that he ever even considered the metaphysical possibility that is the equivalent, in the case of causation, of the metaphysical possibility that there might be no genuinely external physical objects: i.e. the possibility that the whole order of the world might be, as it were, a continuous fluke; or, in other words, the possibility that the regularity theory of causation might be true as an ontological doctrine. There's no evidence that he ever considered the view that he is so famous for holding, according to which causation

---

[43] Again: 'every simple impression is attended with a correspondent idea, and every simple idea with a correspondent impression'; and this 'constant conjunction, in such an infinite number of instances, can never arise from chance; but *clearly proves a dependence* of the impressions on the ideas, or of the ideas on the impressions' (4–5/1.1.1.8).

[44] 93/1.3.6.15. Here I draw on Strawson 1989: ch. 15.

is nothing more than regular succession or constant conjunction.[45] It is, after all, a far, far more bizarre idea than the idealist idea that objects might be nothing but experiences. For even if objects are nothing but experiences, their orderly behaviour stands as much in need of explanation as it does if they are physical objects as ordinarily conceived.[46]

Consider some remarks by Philo, Hume's spokesman in the *Dialogues*:

How could things have been as they are, were there not an original, inherent principle of order somewhere, in thought or in matter? . . . Chance has no place on any hypothesis, sceptical or religious. Everything is surely governed by steady, inviolable laws. And were the inmost essence of things laid open to us, we should then discover a scene, of which, at present, we can have no idea. Instead of admiring the order of natural beings, we should clearly see, that it was absolutely impossible for them, in the smallest article, ever to admit of any other disposition. (174–5/76–7)

'Tis observed by arithmeticians, that the products of 9 compose always 9 or some lesser product of 9, if you add together all the characters, of which any of the former products are composed. Thus, of 18, 27, 36, which are products of 9, you make 9 by adding 1 to 8, 2 to 7, 3 to 6. Thus 369, is a product also of nine; and if you add 3, 6, and 9, you make 18, a lesser product of 9. To a superficial observer, so wonderful a regularity may be admir'd as the effect either of chance, or design; but a skillful algebraist immediately concludes it to be the work of necessity, and demonstrates, that it must for ever result from the nature of these numbers. Is it not probable, I ask, that the whole economy of the universe is conducted by a like necessity . . . ? And instead of admiring the order of natural beings, may it not happen, that, could we penetrate into the intimate nature of bodies, we should clearly see why it was absolutely impossible, they could ever admit of any other disposition? (191/93)

These aren't the views of a regularity theorist. They're Hume's views, dramatically presented, and too little known.[47]

---

[45] See e.g. Kripke 1982: 67: 'If Hume is right, even if God were to look at [two causally related] events, he would discern nothing relating them other than that one succeeds the other.'

[46] Cf. Strawson 1989: 219–20.

[47] Here Hume has abandoned his ardor-of-youth endorsement of extreme, Wittgensteinian global subjectivism about necessity (166/1.3.14.23), while retaining the idea, also found in that paragraph, that natural necessity is like mathematical necessity. See p. 115 n. 16 below.

Some say that it can't be proved that Philo is Hume's spokesman. I'll shortly argue that we don't need to prove this to take the *Dialogues* to provide further powerful evidence that Hume isn't a regularity theorist. But I think we have all the proof we need. Philo dominates the *Dialogues*, and is the representative sceptic. No one denies that he's the best candidate. In a letter Hume imagines Gilbert Elliot and himself writing a dialogue together. He casts Elliot as Cleanthes, and then says of himself 'I should have taken on me the character of Philo, in the Dialogue, which you'll own I could have supported naturally enough' (1751: 154). In another letter he wrote 'In every dialogue, no more than one person can be supposed to represent the author' (1753: 173).

There are perhaps two main reasons why the identification of Hume with Philo has been disputed. The first is that the clever mischief of Philo's apparent concession that there is a god (in Part XII of the *Dialogues*) has been widely misunderstood. Hume was certainly an agnostic, and he was certainly an atheist with respect to the Christian God as standardly defined, but there is nothing he can't accept in Philo's brilliant argument in Part XII.[48]

The second main reason why the identification of Philo with Hume has long been found uncomfortable is precisely that Philo talks in a realist fashion about natural or objective necessity, while granting that its nature is entirely unknowable. On the present view of Hume, however, this is no objection. It confirms the acceptability of the identification, rather than constituting an objection to it. Philo, like Hume, believes in the existence of some principle of order given which the universe is regular in the way that it is, while holding that we know nothing about its ultimate nature.

Suppose we try the contrary hypothesis: Philo isn't Hume, and Hume really does hold the view that causation is nothing but regularity.

---

[48] Philo's long speech beginning 'All men of sound reason . . .' is particularly relevant (D217–19/119–21). Here his understanding of the deity turns out—as he explicitly says—to include nothing that any atheist can possibly wish to disagree with. It also constitutes a further affirmation of causal realism.

A bewildering question arises: Why does Hume allow Philo to assume the intelligibility (and assert the truth) of some form of objective necessity thesis without any challenge? If Hume really holds, and particularly cherishes, the view that causation is nothing but constant conjunction or regular succession, why doesn't he ever put any of his supposed arguments for this view into anyone's mouth in the *Dialogues*, even where the context invites it?

Don't say that the *Dialogues* is marginal to Hume's main work in philosophy (this is sometimes assumed to be the case, in the wake of a tradition of interpretation that simply can't accommodate the *Dialogues*). It is, if anything, the jewel at the centre, brilliant in itself, and particularly treasured by Hume. Shortly before he died he wrote to his publisher about the *Dialogues*: 'Some of my friends flatter me, that it is the best thing I ever wrote' (1776: 323).

It should be added that it isn't a late work, as some suppose. Hume began work on it in 1749, shortly after the first edition of the *Enquiry* was published in 1748. He reworked it at various times, was too cautious to publish it during his life, but took particular care to ensure that it would be published after his death.

1.6 Hume and Wittgenstein

I've noted the parallel between the strict empiricist approach to physical objects and the strict empiricist approach to causation, pointing out that Hume can't be arguing for the thesis that there's definitely no such thing as causation as ordinarily conceived of. He's certainly not arguing the parallel thesis for objects, and claiming that objects definitely don't exist in so far as they're supposed to be different from experiences. In the case of objects, he's working out the sceptical arguments and establishing the limits to knowledge. We shouldn't suppose that he's doing something different in the case of causation, pursuing a positive metaphysical programme and arguing that causation is definitely just constant conjunction. Placed in historical context, his scepticism with respect to knowledge of objects is relatively familiar, while his scepticism with respect to knowledge of causation is more original, although it's certainly not unanticipated (by Locke, among others), and is vividly prepared for by Berkeley.[49]

Many have thought that Hume argues from epistemology to semantics to ontology—from 'can't know x' to 'can't mean x' to 'x doesn't (and can't) exist'. He doesn't. Many have thought that it's a good line of argument. It isn't. Some think it's the cornerstone of rigorous empiricism. It isn't. The problem is not merely that it's an invalid form of argument (that's a relatively minor defect, if one's trying to be a radical empiricist). The major defect is that it leads, as I have argued, to gross epistemological immodesty—false certainty—and mad metaphysics.

Those who think that Hume positively endorses some sort of idealism about objects, and some sort of regularity thesis about causation, may resemble those who think that Wittgenstein denies the reality of the sensation of pain. Consider the result of substituting 'regular succession' for 'pain-behaviour', and 'causation' for 'sensation', in §304 of Wittgenstein's *Philosophical Investigations*. Wittgenstein's imaginary interlocutor speaks first:

—But you will surely admit that there is a difference between regular succession accompanied by [or involving] causation and regular succession without any causation?
—Admit it [replies Wittgenstein]? What greater difference could there be?
—And yet you again and again reach the conclusion that the causation itself is a *nothing*.
—Not at all. . . . The conclusion was only that a *nothing* would serve just as well as a *something* about which nothing could be said.

It seems to me that Wittgenstein is muddled, and implausibly extreme, as compared with Hume (whom Wittgenstein once said he could not read, because he—Hume—was so muddled). Nevertheless, this passage, with these substitutions, expresses part of Hume's view reasonably well. There's no denial of the existence of (real) causation, any more than there is of sensations.

---

[49] See e.g. *Essay* §§4.2.10–16, 22, 28–9. On the special implausibility of combining realism about physical objects with a regularity theory of causation, see Strawson 1987: 397–402. Berkeley was a regularity theorist with respect to physical objects; see e.g. Strawson 1989: 44–7, 257–61 ('Cartoon-film causation').

One may also substitute 'external object' for 'sensation':

—And yet you again and again reach the conclusion that the external object itself is a *nothing*.

—Not at all. . . . The conclusion was only that a ***nothing*** would serve just as well as a *something* about which nothing could be said.[50]

---

[50]   In full, the final response runs as follows: 'Not at all. It is not a *something*, but it is not a *nothing* either! The conclusion was only that a *nothing* would serve just as well as a something about which nothing could be said.' The omitted sentence is a rhetorically dramatic contradiction (that's why it ends with an exclamation mark). One could gloss the contradictory sentence by saying that its claim is that pain-sensation (or causation, or a world of external objects) is not a something of which one can give any positively descriptive account in (public) language, or (alternatively) on the terms of the theory of ideas.

PART 2

Mind, Self, and Person

There is no question in philosophy more abstruse than that
concerning identity, and the nature of the uniting principle, which
constitutes a person . . . the metaphysical question of the identity of a
thinking substance.

Hume 1739: 189, 190/1.4.2.6, 1.4.2.9

2.1 Introduction

In Section 1.4.6 of the *Treatise*, David Hume applies his empiricist principles to the idea of the mind or self. He concludes that

the true idea of the human mind is to consider it as a system of different perceptions
or different existences.[1]

The mind or self, conceived of in this way, isn't a single, continuously
existing, persisting thing. It is, rather, a compound, gappy thing, a 'bundle'
of experiences, a bundle of mental occurrences—a bundle of 'perceptions'.

Within a year, Hume sees that he can't maintain the view that this is the
true idea of the mind, although his empiricist principles commit him to the
view that it is. Or rather, he sees that it's not the idea of the mind that he's
worked with in his philosophy, although his empiricist principles commit
him to working with no other. This is his problem: the empiricistically
'true' idea of the mind isn't consistent with his philosophical commitments
and presuppositions considered as a whole.

---

[1] 261/§19. More fully, 'as to *causation*; we may observe, that the true idea of the human
mind, is to consider it as a system of different perceptions or different existences, which are
link'd together by the relation of cause and effect and mutually produce, destroy, influence,
and modify each other'.

He finds himself unable to solve this problem, and he says so, most ingenuously, in the Appendix to the *Treatise*. He doesn't withdraw the metaphysical claim that all there is to the mind or self, in reality, is a bundle of perceptions or experiences, for this is a claim he never made. Nor does he change his view about what the 'true' idea of the mind or self is, given his empiricist principles. He doesn't change his mind about the content of the properly warranted, clear and distinct idea of the mind or self, the idea of the mind or self that is available for legitimate use in an empiricist philosophy that seeks to make knowledge claims. For he can't see anything wrong with it, given his empiricist principles.

This, again, is his problem. His philosophy relies—essentially—on a richer idea of the mind or self than his empiricist principles allow him. When he tries to reconcile the empiricistically 'true' (fully empirically warranted) idea of the mind with certain other claims he makes about how the mind works—claims that underpin his whole philosophy—his 'hopes vanish' (635/App§20). The empiricist account can't give him what he needs. It can't provide something whose existence is a fundamental presupposition of his overall theory. He realizes that he has throughout his philosophy made use of—presupposed—a notion of the mind or self that is open to the objection that it is not legitimate by his own lights.

Is he right? I believe he is. I think that what happens to Hume in the Appendix is something that not uncommonly happens when people have finished a piece of theoretical work: they see that there is an error or inconsistency in the position. The worst thing about it is that it's an error or inconsistency that they could hardly have failed to notice if it hadn't been possible for them to pursue many of their theoretical goals in spite of it.[2]

Must any account of Hume's discussion of the mind or self show that he's right to think that he faces a major difficulty, if it is to be convincing? I think so, but there's no need to press the point. What is surely true is that an account that shows that he's right in the Appendix is greatly to be

---

[2] This happens to the cleverest people. Sometimes they notice it themselves—perhaps this is Hume's case. Sometimes someone else brings it to their attention (Frege has Russell, Wittgenstein has Ramsey and Sraffa, Kant has Hume). There's nothing like publication for revealing an error to an author—for forcing into full consciousness a theoretical problem that has been shifting about in the shadows of the mind, but has never been properly faced. This experience has a very distinctive phenomenology.

preferred to one that doesn't. For if anyone has a clear grasp of what Hume's theory amounts to and entails, it's Hume himself. He doesn't take back his confession of failure at any later point in his career, and in the first *Enquiry* he firmly endorses the claim that prompts the confession of failure, when, in his only direct reference to the abandoned problem, he observes, briefly but decisively, that

it is evident that there is a principle of connexion between the different thoughts or ideas of the mind. (23/3.1)

Here he refers to a real connection of precisely the sort that the empiricistically 'true idea' of the human mind can't countenance.[3] It's the same 'principle of connexion' that he refers to in the Appendix, the principle of connection that, he says, makes 'my hopes vanish . . . when I proceed to explain' it (635/App§20). The problem is that he can't explain it on the terms of his empiricist theory of ideas, and, in particular, his empiricist account of the mind.

I'll discuss the Appendix in Part 3. Here in Part 2 I'll lay out the bundle account of the mind (or self or person), which Hume formulates in a number of different ways. Two points are worth making before beginning.

The first is that in this discussion Hume uses the word 'person' interchangeably with the words 'mind' and 'self', and takes 'person' to have a merely mental reference, along with the expressions 'thinking person' and 'thinking principle'.[4] There's a persistent looseness in the way he moves between these terms, and sometimes he uses them with somewhat different force. I don't, however, think that one needs to try to remove the looseness. I'll leave it in place, moving between the terms as he does and as the context suggests, speaking mainly of mind and self, because 'person' is now standardly used to refer to a human being considered as a whole.[5]

---

[3] On Hume's use of 'connexion' see above p. 27 n. 43.

[4] This is why he discusses the topic under the heading 'Of personal identity', in a way that can seem odd given the present-day sense of 'person'.

[5] For evidence of interchangeability, see e.g. 251/§2, 253/§5, 262/§20, 'self or person'; 260/§17, 'mind or thinking person'; 260/§18, 'mind or thinking principle'. As Pike says, 'When Hume uses the term . . . "person", he generally means to be referring only to the mind' (1967: 161).

The second point flows from the first. Given that Hume is considering us specifically as mental subjects, rather than as whole human beings, his uninhibited use of 'our' in phrases like 'our particular perceptions' (252/§ 3) or 'our successive perceptions' (636/App§20) may seem to presuppose the very reality that it seeks [a] to put in question and [b] to explain our belief in. It may seem to presuppose the reality of a persisting self that is the continuing subject of all these successive experiences; it may seem to presuppose the view that the belief in such a persisting self is in fact correct, even as it seeks to show that such a belief isn't justified. At the very least, it seems that Hume must be speaking loosely, when he uses 'our' in this way, given that it is precisely the question of the mental self's identity through time that is at issue.

This troubled Merian in 1793, who put the following question to Hume:

What is the meaning in your mind and your mouth of these personal pronouns which you cannot prevent yourself from continually using, and without which you would not know either to think or to express your thoughts, *me*, *I*, *we*, etc? (1793: 190)

Merian's point is that the personal pronouns seem to have no proper reference, given the bundle account of the mind; many others have made similar objections. But there's no great difficulty here for Hume. It's not hard to understand what he's saying. For practical purposes of interpretation we won't go wrong if we give his uses of 'our' a whole-human-being reading, a reading that posits a persisting human being but doesn't presuppose any persisting inner subject. That said, one can put things more accurately by saying that what phrases like 'our successive experiences' (non-question-beggingly) do, when Hume employs them in the framework of his discussion of the empirical content of the idea of personal identity, is to characterize how things seem to the (possibly very short-lived) subject of any given experience, from the perspective of that experience, given that that subject already has the belief in a persisting self, a sense of itself as a persisting something that has and has had many successive experiences.

This reply to Merian assumes something that should I think be obvious, but has been widely doubted: it assumes that Hume takes it that any experience, however short-lived, has a subject. I will turn to this point in 2.3 (see also 2.14).

2.2 'Perception', 'experience'

In one of the most famous passages in philosophy, Hume writes that

when I enter most intimately into what I call *myself* I always stumble on some particular perception or other . . . and never can observe anything but the perception. (252/§3)

This has led many to believe that his bundle account of the mind incorporates the claim that an experience—a conscious mental episode, a thought or sensation, a 'perception' in Hume's terms—can occur even when there is no experiencer: no subject of experience for whom that experience is an experience; no sort of subjective presence at all. Some philosophers, it seems, have even endorsed such a theory. Hume, however, never entertains any such view, which is sometimes now known as the 'no ownership' view. This is not surprising, because there is a fundamental sense in which it's incoherent.[6]

I'll say more about this in the next section. First, a terminological provision: where Hume uses the word 'perception' to denote a mental occurrence I'll usually use the word 'experience' (the count noun). The generality of 'experience' in present-day use corresponds very well to the generality of Hume's use of 'perception', and it seems a good idea, when discussing Hume, to try to suspend some of the old interpretative assumptions (reflexes) that are coded so deeply into the word 'perception'. When 'perception' occurs in quotations from Hume in Part 2, I'll regularly replace it by '[experience]', the square brackets marking the fact that I have made the substitution.

In Hume's principal use of the term 'perception' all perceptions are conscious by definition, in so far as they're concretely existing entities[7]

---

[6]   The idea that an experience might occur without any subject—in the sense of subjective presence—at all is not endorsed by Buddhists; nor is it supported by the claim that we may do better, in the end, to speak of 'subjectivity' than 'subject' (see 2.14 below). Certainly it has nothing to do with the 'no ownership' view discussed by P. F. Strawson, and rightly criticized by him as incoherent (1959: 94–99). In 2.8 below I consider one possible sense in which Hume can be said to espouse a version of the 'no ownership' view.

[7]   For all practical purposes one can take 'concretely existing entities' to mean entities occurring or existing in time. Whatever these concretely existing entities are, they're not 'abstract entities' like numbers or concepts.

at all.[8] The same goes for experiences in ordinary current usage. Conscious experiences divide into two types, for Hume: 'impressions', which are episodes of feeling or sensory experience, and 'ideas', which are episodes of consciously entertaining or deploying concepts, for example when we engage in conscious thought.[9] It follows that we must in replacing 'perception' by 'experience' allow that episodes of conscious thought and of consciously entertaining ideas are experiences, just as episodes of sensing and feeling are. This, however, is hardly a problem, for they are. There's more to the overall phenomenological character of our experience than just sense/feeling experience (taking this term to cover not only all sensory experience, interoceptive and exteroceptive, but also all mood and emotion and mental-image-involving experience). We can't possibly give a full characterization of the total experiential character of our experience from moment to moment by referring only to sense/feeling experience. There's also such a thing as the experience of thought, of understanding mathematics, a metaphor, and so on. We can put this by saying that there is, in addition to sense/feeling phenomenology, cognitive phenomenology. Consider your experience as you read this sentence now, and the next. You can't give a full account of it—of the total, overall character of what it is like to be you, experientially, right now—just by reference to feeling-experience.[10] 'Experience consists not only of feelings, but also of judgements' (Kant 1788: 14).

[8] I say 'principal usage' because Hume first introduces the word 'perception' in the *Treatise* in a way that suggests that perceptions are not themselves conscious episodes at all, but rather things that '*strike upon* the mind, and *make their way into* our thought or consciousness', things that '*enter*' the mind (1/1.1.1.1, 190/1.4.2.7) and exist independently of consciousness in such a way that they can be '*excited by*' doing something like reading the *Treatise*. This usage ceases in the First *Enquiry*, where 'perception' is only ever used to mean what it is usually used to mean in the *Treatise*: an actual conscious episode.

[9] Simply put, the difference between impressions and ideas is the difference between feeling and thinking, and as Hume says, 'every one of himself will readily perceive the difference betwixt feeling and thinking' (1/1.1.1.1). Hume's way of making the distinction has been heavily criticized, but is in fact thoroughly viable. For a good discussion see Everson 1988. See also Craig 1986.

[10] There was a time—which is perhaps now passing—when most analytic philosophers denied this claim. For a defence, see e.g. James 1890: 1.245–46, Strawson 2011a. Moore puts the point as follows: 'I will now utter certain words which form a sentence: these words, for instance: Twice two are four. Now, when I say these words, you not only hear *them*—the words—you *also* understand what they mean. That is to say, something happens in your minds—some act of consciousness—*over and above* the hearing of the words, some act of consciousness which may be called the understanding of their meaning' (1910: 57).

The replacement of 'perception' by 'experience' may cause some stumbling at various points. Some may find it displeasing. I think this may be philosophically helpful. But anyone who is suspicious should feel free to replace either word by the other in any relevant context.

There's a natural and systematic ambiguity built into terms like 'perception', 'impression', 'idea', and 'experience', which it's important to note. A perception or experience can be a particular mental episode occurring at a particular time, a particular conscious mental occurrence. This is the most natural use of the word. It's how I use it in the last two paragraphs, and it's how Hume almost always uses it in the parts of his book that principally concern us now, i.e. 'Of personal identity' (section 1.4.6 of the *Treatise*), paragraphs 10–21 of the Appendix to the *Treatise*, and paragraph 28 of the *Abstract*.[11] 'Perception' or 'experience' can also, however, be used to refer to a *type* of mental episode or mental content, not a particular individual *token* mental episode or content occurring at a particular time. In fact Hume is more likely to use the words 'idea' and 'impression' than the word 'perception', when he has types of mental content rather than occurrent experiences in mind, but there are also occasions when he uses 'perception' when he has types of mental content in mind.[12]

The ambiguity isn't troublesome so long as one remains aware of it. The same ambiguity is found in all other similar terms (Locke's and Berkeley's 'ideas'; Arnauld's and Leibniz's 'perceptions'; Kant's 'representations' or 'presentations' or 'cognitions', i.e. his count-noun use of the term *Erkenntnis*; 'thoughts', 'sensations', and so on). Most of the time we deal with it automatically. When someone talks of a thought, for example, they may mean an actual mental episode that occurs at a particular place and time—I think *that water is wet* here and now—or they may mean something that is arguably no less a single and particular entity, although it's something that you and I and thousands of others can all think at different times and places, centuries and continents apart: *the thought that water is wet*. In the first use, a thought is a concretely occurring, clockable item.[13] It is a particular occurrence of mental content, a particular instance or 'token' of thought.

---

[11] Of fifty-nine occurrences of the word 'perception' in these passages, only one is (arguably) a content-type use. See p. 80 n. 82 below.

[12] He uses 'idea' and 'impression' in both ways in 'Of personal identity', and sometimes occurrences of the words can be read both ways. See e.g. the first occurrence of 'impression' (251/§2).

[13] I'm assuming that materialism is true for purposes of discussion.

In the second use it's a content-*type*, as remarked. It is, as some philosophers like to say, an 'abstract entity', not a concrete clockable item at all. Exactly the same is true in the case of sensations. There are actual sensations and types of sensations.

In one sense, then (the concrete-item sense), it's impossible for you and I to have the same thought or sensation or experience. In another sense (the content-type sense), nothing is easier. The distinction is no more puzzling than the distinction between qualitative identity and numerical identity,[14] of which it's a special case. We do, however, need to bear it in mind, because error can arise from overlooking it.[15]

Note that when I speak of an 'occurrence of content' I'm using the word 'content' to mean something wholly concrete. I'm using it to mean the actual overall occurrent phenomenological character of an experience: that which makes it true to say that now things are like *this* for the experiencer, experientially, and that a second later they're different and are like *this* instead. This use of 'content' is non-standard in present-day philosophy of mind, but it's readily intelligible and wholly Humean. I take it that such concretely occurring experiential content is 'narrow' content, in the modern idiom, purely 'internal' content—whatever you want to call the thing whose existence is the most certain of all things and which includes conscious entertainings of thoughts as much as sensory contents. It is experiential 'what-it's-likeness', if you wish, something that occurs in particular times and places, and involves both sense/feeling phenomenology and cognitive phenomenology (meaning-experience, understanding-experience).

2.3 'An experience is impossible without an experiencer'[16]

An individual experience or 'perception' isn't just a content-type (an impression content-type or an idea content-type). In most of Hume's uses of the term, and in almost all of the uses in the passages that now most concern us, a perception is an actual happening, an occurrent, clockable, conscious

---

[14] Mentioned by Hume in 1.3. (69/1.3.1.1).

[15] For a possible case of this, see pp. 139–40 below.

[16] Frege 1918: 27. One can know this to be true prior to and independently of any other metaphysical commitments (see e.g. Strawson 1994: 129–33).

event of feeling or thinking. A perception, in other words, is a *perceiving*, an actual episode of perceiving; an experience is an *experiencing*, an actual episode of experiencing. More simply, a perception is—a *perception*! An experience is—an *experience*! To hear these tautologies in the right way is to see that the idea that there could be an experience (perception) without an experienc*er* (perceiv*er*) is like the idea that there could be a square without sides, let alone four sides, or a dent without a surface. It's a necessary truth that an experience entails an experiencer, a subject of experience, as many have observed. It's a truth no less secure (more secure?) than 2 + 2 = 4. For experience is necessarily experience-*for*-someone-or-something, however this someone-or-something is further characterized. 'An experience is impossible without an experiencer.'[17]

I'll call this necessary truth the *Experience/Experiencer* thesis. I've defended it elsewhere,[18] and will take it for granted here. Even when Hume is at the furthest, Cartesian point of his doubt, in the last section of Book 1 of the *Treatise*, the one thing he plainly and rightly doesn't doubt (along with the existence of experiences) is the existence of the subject of experience that he is in the depths of his doubt. In the deepest depths of his doubt, he writes 'I . . . can look upon no opinion even as more probable or likely than another', he writes. 'Where am I, or what? From what causes do I derive my existence?' (268–9/1.4.7.8) The only thing that's not in question at this point is his own present existence and the existence of his experiences.[19]

Whatever Hume's target is in 'Of personal identity', then, it isn't belief in the existence of subjects of experience. They exist as certainly as experiences do. Experiences have to be had—experienced—to exist, and a subject exists even if only one experience exists. We have to do with 'a thinking being', i.e. an experiencing being, even when we consider a mind 'reduc'd even below the life of an oyster', a mind that has 'only one [experience], as of thirst or hunger' (634/App§16).

---

[17]   For a recent expression of the view, see Shoemaker 1986: 10: 'I am of course taking it as an obvious conceptual truth that an experiencing is necessarily an experiencing by a subject of experience, and involves that subject as intimately as a branch-bending involves a branch'.

[18]   Strawson 1994: 129–33; more recently, Strawson 2009: 268–76.

[19]   Some may think Lichtenberg's objection to Descartes—that Descartes should have said only 'it thinks', not 'I think'—is relevant. In fact it's no more apposite here than it is as an objection to Descartes (see e.g. Strawson 2009: 140).

Thomas Reid assumes that a subject of experience or thinking being must be a persisting thing. He also assumes that it must be something ontically over and above any episode of experience. He is, accordingly, one of the first of many who wrongly represent Hume as putting forward the view that 'the mind is only a succession of ideas and impressions *without any subject*', and 'that sensation and thought may be *without a thinking being*' (1764: 32, 33 (2§6)). For he takes it, first, that a subject or thinking being must be an uninterruptedly persisting thing—something whose existence is indeed ruled out by a bundle account of the mind. He also takes it that it must be something ontologically distinct from any experiences—ideas and impressions—it may have; something which is, again, ruled out by a bundle account of the mind.

He duly produces an early version of the popular but irrelevant objection that a series of experiences can't itself be a subject of experience:

But who is the *I* that has this memory and consciousness of a succession of ideas and impressions? Why, it is nothing but that succession itself.... This succession of ideas and impressions, not only remembers and is conscious, but... it judges, reasons, affirms, denies; nay... it eats and drinks, and is sometimes merry, and sometimes sad. If these things can be ascribed to a succession of ideas and impressions, in a consistency with common sense, I should be very glad to know what is nonsense. (1785: 473–4 (§6.5))

In a similar vein, MacNabb asks the 'hexametrical question': 'How can a series of conscious thoughts be aware of itself as a series?' (1951: 251).

The reply is that each experience, of course, and necessarily, involves a subject of experience, a subject that experiences what is experienced in that experience.[20] Hume's target isn't belief in the existence of subjects of experience of any sort or duration whatever. He remains certain of the existence of two things at the furthest point of his doubt. First, the thing he is himself in the moment of doubt, the subject of experience, whatever its nature; secondly, the experiencing currently occurring in his field of consciousness. The extreme sceptical thought is that there is nothing more to his existence than the experiencing that is currently occurring. That experiencing does of course involve an experiencer. One can't, however, know that the experiencer has any sort of existence independently of the experiencing. But to say that one can't know that the experiencer has any

---

[20] As for the eating and drinking, Hume is talking about the mental subject.

existence independently of the experiencing is not to say that there might somehow be 'mere experiential content', without it being content *for* any experiencing entity at all (see further 2.14 below).

Given that Hume's target isn't belief in the *existence* of a subject of experience, what is it? He says what it is, very plainly, right at the start of his discussion of personal identity. It's a certain highly specific substantive metaphysical view about the *nature* of the self or subject of experience, together with a correlative epistemological claim about what can be known about its nature.[21] It's the metaphysical view, routine if not universal at the time, that the self or subject is something that has 'perfect identity and simplicity' and 'continue[s] invariably the same, through the whole course of our lives'; together with the epistemological view that this is something that we can know to be the case (251/§§1–2). It's the view of the mind or self or soul or subject as

[+A]   a thing that has long-term existence
[+B]   a diachronically non-compound thing
[+C]   a diachronically continuous thing
[+D]   a diachronically unchanging thing
[+E]   a synchronically non-compound thing.

[+A] is taken for granted by the philosophers of the time, as already remarked, [+B], [+C], and [+D] represent the 'perfect identity' claim, with [+D] stressing the 'invariableness' claim, and [+E] backs up [+B] in representing the 'perfect simplicity' or indivisibility claim considered apart from the diachronic issue of 'identity'.[22] Note that all five claims are intended to be claims about the supposed *substantial nature* of the mind or self. Thus [+D] doesn't claim that there are no changes in the mind's or self's experiences over time, only that the mind or self or soul remains, as regards its substance, the same unchanging thing over time.[23]

—This may be Hume's main target, but I'm not convinced that he isn't arguing for some form of the 'no ownership' view—some form of the view that experiences

---

[21] Kant has the same target in the Paralogisms (Kant 1781/7: A341–405/B399–432).

[22] 'Identity' simply means 'diachronic identity' in the personal identity debate of the time—for Locke, Hume (see especially 201/1.4.2.29), Kant, and many others. Note that [+E] is the topic of Kant's Second Paralogism, [+B], [+C], and [+D] are the topic of his Third.

[23] See 2.11 below. The list may seem to contain redundancy, but I will later consider four views that, taken collectively, disagree about all of [+A] to [+E].

can exist without an experiencer existing. What about his claim that '[experiences] . . . may be consider'd as separately existent, and may exist separately', for example? (233/1.4.5.5)

To say that experiences may be considered as separately existent, and may exist separately, is in no way to say or suggest—incoherently—that they can exist without involving a subject. It is, to repeat, a necessary truth, a dent/surface truth, that an experience involves a subject of experience— that an experien*cing* involves an experien*cer* in some ineliminable sense. (I consider the objection that there may be only subjectivity, not a subject, in section 2.14.) If experiences do exist separately in the way imagined, all that follows is that there are as many subjects of experience as there are numerically distinct experiences. It's not: no self or subject in any sense at all. It's just: no persisting self or subject—let alone a substantially simple, substantially immutable subject.[24]

This is a version of the 'Transience' view of mental selves or subjects that attracts the William James of *The Principles of Psychology* and many others, including Buddhists, and me.[25] Be that as it may, Hume's claim here is simply that when it comes to the self, all we're actually given in experience is a series of experiences which may (for all that we're given in experience) exist separately from each other, e.g. without being states of a single continuing entity. His point is empiricist and epistemological. It is that we can't know that this isn't how things actually are, when it comes to the question of the subject of experience or self, because this is all that is clearly given to us in experience, on his empiricist principles.[26]

---

[24] Note that a perception that counts as a single perception in so far as it's 'complex' (a complex impression of an apple, for example (2/1.1.1.2), or simultaneous experience of phthalo green + taste of manna + the sound of a krumhorn) can also be said to consist of several distinct perceptions, in Hume's terms. In fact what we naturally think of as an entirely simple perception—an experience of a uniformly coloured expanse, say—already involves many small perceptions, in Hume's terms, and is in that sense complex. But there is of course only one perceiver or subject of any complex perception: it can't constitute *a* complex perception at all, i.e. a single complex perception, unless all the constituent impressions or ideas are experienced together in a way that strictly—logically—requires a single experiencer. In 1.4.6 Hume talks of perceptions 'mingling' (253/§4) and being 'cotemporary' (259/§16), and in the Appendix he suggests that he may come upon more than one perception at a given time, when he turns his reflection on himself (634/App§15). Here again, we are to imagine a single complex experience being had by a single experiencer.

[25] We all think that this may be the best thing to say if one is going to talk about selves at all. See e.g. James 1890: 1.338–42, 400–01.

[26] It may be said that the 'streamlike' character of our experience of consciousness provides direct experiential evidence for continuity (see e.g. Dainton 2008). I disagree, but this is a

The point can be restated in semantic terms in a way that is by now familiar. When, with Hume, we undertake the task of trying to establish the precise content of terms or concepts suitable for use in philosophy, we are bound to accept the stringent constraints that the proper practice of philosophy imposes on us. We are bound to accept the empiricist principle that no term like 'self' (no concept of self) can be employed in philosophy in a fully legitimate and unproblematic way—and, in particular, in such a way that it can be employed in knowledge claims—unless it can establish its origin in experience in a certain, very direct manner: it must be 'copied' from impressions (see p. 6 n. 12). No concept of the self suitable for unrestricted use in philosophy can have any more content than is delivered by impressions. That is why Hume says that 'the true idea of the human mind is to consider it as a system of different [experiences] or different existences' (261/§19). This is the only positively descriptively contentful idea of the mind we can make free use of in philosophy when claiming any knowledge of the nature of the mind, although we can of course freely refer to the mind in (for example) pointing out that its 'essence . . . is unknown to us' (xvii/Int§8).[27]

topic for another time. Note that even William James, the originator of the term 'stream of consciousness', favoured the many experiences/many subjects view on empiricist grounds in his *Principles of Psychology* (see e.g. 1890: 1.400–1). Note also that the (fully Humean) use of 'we' and 'us' here can be understood in the way proposed on p. 36 above: thus suppose that the experiences that each of us speaks of as 'my' experiences are in fact experiences had successively by many different subjects (associated with a single human being). In that case we may say that the referent of 'my' is strictly speaking the subject of the experience that is then occurring, who falsely thinks that he or she has been the subject of many other experiences. This is in fact exactly what the bundle theory asserts, considered as an outright metaphysical proposal. The present point is that there is no difficulty in using 'we' and 'us' (or 'I' and 'me') to express the theory.

[27] One could put the point by saying that the 'true' idea of the human mind captures the essence of the mind—*within* the philosophical framework of ideas constituted by empirically warranted ideas. But it doesn't capture the essence of the mind *überhaupt*; that is unknown. In exactly the same way Hume's 'exact' or 'precise definition of cause and effect' (169/1.3.14.30) captures the 'true meaning' of expressions like 'a necessary connexion betwixt objects' (162/1.3.14.14) within the framework of empirically warranted ideas, even while the actual 'operating principle of objects' (169/1.3.14.29) remains unknown. One could equally well say that the definition captures the *essence* of cause and effect—*within* the empirically warranted framework. Thus with regard to his first definition of cause, Hume says that 'the constant conjunction of objects constitutes the *very essence of cause and effect* . . . as far as we have any notion of that relation' (1.4.5.33/250). With regard to the second definition of cause, he says that 'the *essence of necessity* . . . is that propensity, which custom produces, to pass from an object to the idea of its usual attendant' (165/1.3.14.22). Yes. For this '*necessary connexion* is . . . merely a perception of the mind' (405–6/2.3.1.16). See further 2. 7.

To say that this is the 'true' idea of the human mind is not, however, to say that there may not *be* some sort of continuing self or mind. Hume explicitly allows that there may be (e.g. in 252/§4, discussed in the next section). His realization in the Appendix that his account of personal identity won't do is his realization that he can't really remain agnostic on the matter of the existence of some sort of real continuity, in the case of minds or selves. He realizes that he can't really remain agnostic even inside the official system of his philosophy. He realizes, in other words, that his overall philosophical scheme commits him to—unequivocally presupposes—the existence of some sort of real continuity of mind or self.

2.4 Epistemology, semantics, ontology, and the self

How does the [E]–[S]–[OE] move described in Part 1 (p. 21) come out in the case of the mind or self? As follows:

[E] experiences are all we can *know* of the mind or self or person,

so

[S] a collection of experiences is all we can positively descriptively or empirically warrantedly or clearly and distinctly or philosophically legitimately *mean* by the idea or concept (term) *mind* or *self* or *person*

—given that we take these terms or ideas to denote or refer to something that lasts longer than a single experience (as of course we do); so

[OE] the mind or self or person, *so far as we have any distinct or empirically warranted or philosophically legitimate conception of it*, is just a collection of experiences.

The italicized epistemological qualification is necessary because 'the essence of the mind is . . . unknown to us'. We don't have even 'the most distant notion' of it (§4). All we may legitimately take it to be, within the confines of a properly conducted—rigorously empiricist—philosophy, is a collection of experiences. This, just this, is Hume's claim in 'Of personal identity'.

—How can this be right? Hume plainly says that minds or selves or persons or thinking beings are 'nothing but a bundle or collection of different [experiences]': 'they are the successive [experiences] only, that constitute the mind'. It is a 'chain of causes and effects, which constitute our self or person' (here the 'causes and effects' are particular experiences). A 'composition of . . . [experiences] . . . forms the self'. A 'train . . . of . . . [experiences] . . . compose a mind'. A 'succession of [experiences] . . . constitutes [a] mind or thinking principle'. He could not be more plain: 'what we call a mind, is nothing but a heap or collection of different [experiences], united together by certain relations'. It is a 'connected mass of [experiences], which constitute a thinking being', 'a connected heap of [experiences]'. It is a 'succession of [experiences], which constitutes our self or person'. 'It must be our several particular [experiences], that compose the mind. I say, compose the mind, not belong to it.' Hume is quite plainly making the argument in the simple [E]–[S]–[O] form.[28]

Time to contrapose. Hume can't—provably can't—hold this view, as it's ordinarily understood. It's ruled out by his scepticism, and few, I think, have ever questioned his commitment to 'moderate scepticism': his natural, sensible rejection of claims to know the ultimate nature of concrete things other than experiences. His claim (again) is simply that this is all there is to the mind in so far as we can suppose ourselves to have an empirically warranted idea of it. If there is any one supreme exegetical obligation on commentators who discuss Hume's views on personal identity, it is to provide an account of these quoted passages that doesn't leave Hume holding—claiming to know—that the mind is nothing more than a collection of experiences. For this is to make him a dogmatic metaphysician, as observed in Part 1, not someone who acknowledges that the 'essence of the mind [is] . . . unknown to us'.

It's true that the young Hume bears some responsibility for the misinterpretation that has led some to treat him as an outright ontological bundle theorist. Like many before and after him he liked to express his central, negative epistemological claim in dramatic, positive, ontological terms. This led him later to write 'I was carried away by the heat of youth and invention to publish too precipitately. . . . I have repented my haste a hundred, and a hundred times' (1751: 158). 'I . . . acknowledge . . . a very great mistake in conduct, viz my publishing at all the Treatise of Human

---

[28] 252/§4, 253/§4, 262/§20, 260/§18, 634/App§15, 635/App§20, 207/1.4.2.39 twice, 207/1.4.2.40, 265/1.4.7.3, 658/Abs§28. Note that six of these eleven quotations are from passages where Hume is discussing something else, or summarizing the view and stating it in a particularly compressed form. See also 277/2.1.2.2.

Nature. . . . Above all, the positive air, which prevails in that book, and which may be imputed to the ardor of youth, so much displeases me, that I have not patience to review it' (1754: 187). But the damage was done—although it only began to show its full extent in the nineteenth century. He might have hoped not to be misunderstood, given his plain statement, right at the beginning of the *Treatise*, that the essence of the mind is unknown to us. But that hope was ill-founded.

'The true idea of the human mind, is to *consider it as* a system of different [experiences] or different existences'.[29] What does Hume mean? What idea does he have in mind? He means the idea of the mind that is clear and distinct, and that therefore has fully legitimate employment in philosophy, given his empiricist principles. The unqualified ontological statements are always shorthand for the properly sceptical epistemological claims or epistemologically qualified ontological claims, and they're restated as such when Hume is being more cautious, more aware of possible misunderstanding. When he adverts briefly to the argument of 'Of personal identity' in the *Abstract*, written after Book 1 of the *Treatise*, he sums up its conclusion as follows: the self or soul

as far as we can conceive it, is nothing but a system or train of different [experiences].[30]

Again, when he summarizes the argument for the bundle view in the Appendix to the *Treatise*, written after Book 1 of the *Treatise*, he renders the conclusion of the argument as follows: we have no

notion of . . . [self], *when conceiv'd distinct from* particular [experiences] . . . we have *no notion* of [the mind], distinct from the particular [experiences]. (635/App§§18, 19)

---

[29] 261/§19. The full sentence, already quoted, reads 'As to *causation*; we may observe, that the true idea of the human mind, is to consider it as a system of different perceptions or different existences, which are link'd together by the relation of cause and effect and mutually produce, destroy, influence, and modify each other', and one way to put Hume's problem in the Appendix is to say that it lies in the clause 'link'd together by the relation of cause and effect'. Briefly, he realizes that he needs the real thing, the real connection, not just the constant conjunction that is all that is represented in the empirically respectable 'true idea'. See Part 3.

[30] 657/Abs§28. Another passage in which a laconic ontological formulation is a compression of an epistemological claim occurs in 262/§21: when Hume states that certain sorts of 'relations of ideas . . . *produce* identity, by means of that easy transition they occasion', he means that they produce our belief in identity, our idea that there is identity, not actual (metaphysical) identity.

To say this, or to switch straight from outright ontological mode into epistemological–ontological mode in a single sentence, as he does in 'Of personal identity'—

they are the successive [experiences] only, that constitute the mind; nor have we the most distant notion of the place, where these scenes [the experiences] are represented, or of the materials, of which it is compos'd[31]

—is obviously not to say that the mind is definitely not anything more than a series of perceptions or experiences.

It may be added that Hume's claims are not as strong as many have supposed even when he's firmly on the epistemological/semantic side of things. For when he says that we have no idea or notion of something x (some putative thing x) he doesn't mean that we have no idea or notion of any sort. He means only that we have no 'distinct' or 'perfect' idea of x, no idea that is legitimate or distinct or 'true' according to his theory of ideas and therefore passed for unrestricted use in philosophy.

To see this, consider his transition from 'perfect idea' to 'idea' in an argument that he gives in the section 'Of the immateriality of the soul' that precedes 'Of personal identity':

We have no perfect idea of anything but of [an experience]. A substance is entirely different from [an experience]. We have, therefore, no idea of a substance. (234/1.4.5.6)

This sufficiently shows that when Hume says 'no idea' he doesn't mean 'no idea at all', only no perfect idea, no sufficiently distinct idea, no philosophically respectable idea, no idea that can be used without risk of confusion and error.

Nothing in what follows depends on this particular point, but it's well worth noting, because it's fundamental to Hume interpretation (misinterpretation) across the board.[32]

---

[31] 253/§4; see Craig 1987: 113–14. Given that the word 'it' can't pick up on 'the mind', it must pick up on 'the place', and the place is the mind; not the mind 'as far as we can conceive it', i.e. have a positively contentful conception of it legitimately derived from impressions, but rather, precisely, the mind whose 'essence is . . . unknown to us', the mind considered as it is beyond our capacity to conceive it.

[32] Compare *Enquiry* 21–2/2.9. 'All ideas, especially abstract ones, are naturally faint and obscure: the mind has but a slender hold of them: they are apt to be confounded with other resembling ideas; and when we have often employed any term, though without a distinct meaning, we are apt to imagine it has a determinate idea annexed to it.' It's not that we have no idea at all (although it's true that we have no philosophically respectable idea); it's just that we have no determinate idea. Elsewhere in the *Enquiry*, the strong claim is reasserted in the

—What about the *Abstract*, in which Hume wrote: 'We have no idea of a substance of any kind, since we have no idea but what is derived from some impression, and we have no impression of any substance either material or spiritual' (658/Abs§28)? This seems very clear: it's not just that we have no *perfect* idea; we have no idea *at all*.

Here Hume says that any idea at all must be an empiricistically legitimate idea derived from a suitable impression. Once again, though, he doesn't actually think we have no idea of substance 'of any kind'. In the *Abstract* he makes the same polemical or 'ardor-of-youth' transition—from 'no empiricistically legitimate idea' to 'no idea at all, no idea of any kind'—as he does in the argument just quoted from 1.4.5.6. His basic claim, again, is that we have no suitably evidentially warranted or philosophically legitimate idea of substance, no idea that has any clear positive descriptive content on the terms of his empiricist theory of meaning.[33]

By way of further proof, consider the rather charming move he makes a little later on in 1.4.5. 'This gives me an occasion', he writes,

> to take anew into consideration the question concerning the substance of the soul; and tho' I have condemn'd that question as utterly unintelligible, yet I cannot forbear proposing some farther reflections concerning it. (240/1.4.5.17)

There follow ten pages (240–50/1.4.5.17–33) of brilliant and eminently contentful and intelligible argument *whose possibility depends essentially on there being some sort of thoroughly contentful idea of substance* in play, however imperfect it is. Perhaps this quotation should be pinned above the desk of any aspiring Hume scholar.

Hume ends the discussion as he began it, with a judgement of absolute unintelligibility: 'To pronounce, then, the final decision upon the whole; the question concerning the substance of the soul'—the question which he has

---

discussion of causation: 'as we can have no idea of any thing, which never appeared to our outward sense or inward sentiment, the necessary conclusion seems to be, that we have no idea of connexion or power at all, and that these words are absolutely without any meaning, when employed either in philosophical reasonings, or common life' (74/7.26). The point is the same: we have no genuinely descriptively contentful conception of real connection in the objects at all.

[33] It's striking that some commentators claim that Hume holds both that we have no idea of substance and that a perception (of which we have a 'perfect idea' 234/1.4.5.5) is a substance.

just been discussing at length with intense, substantive, and entirely mean-ingful, i.e. wholly intelligible, brilliance—'is absolutely unintelligible'.[34]

There's a mass of further evidence that when Hume says that we have no idea of something he doesn't mean that we have no idea at all, only that we have no clear and distinct idea, no idea that can be used to make knowledge claims in philosophy, no idea or notion that is not in some way imperfect, deficient, indistinct, inexact, merely relative, inaccurate, inadequate, imprecise, loose, uncertain, confused, indeterminate, obscure, implicit, distant, vulgar, 'fiction'-involving.[35] He can't think that all ideas that are defective in these ways fail to be ideas (mental elements) at all—that they fail to have any content of any sort.

It's not just that he calls them 'ideas', constantly using 'idea' in the natural wider sense (see p. 9) that allows that ideas can exist without being 'perfect', without being empirically respectable. A further point is this: if he thought that they had no content, he'd have to concede that they all have exactly the same content—i.e. no content at all. (Or else, perhaps, a single homogeneous fuzziness content common to all of them.) But he certainly doesn't think this. He doesn't think that all 'fictions' (i.e. empiri-cal-evidence-transcending hypotheses) and imprecisions have exactly the same content, in so far as they have content at all. The fiction-involving (empirical-evidence-transcending) belief in external objects doesn't have exactly the same content as the fiction-involving (empirical-evidence-transcending) belief in the self, although they have important structural features in common, any more than it has exactly the same content as the fiction-involving (empirical-evidence-transcending) belief in causal neces-sity. The 'absolutely unintelligible' notion of the substance of the soul doesn't have exactly the same content as the 'unintelligible' notion of the

---

[34] 250/1.4.5.33. It's plain from context that this 'absolutely unintelligible' idea of substance isn't the idea of substance he has in mind when he says, early in the *Treatise*, that we have 'no idea of substance, distinct from that of a collection of particular qualities, nor have we any other meaning when we either talk or reason concerning it' (16/1.1.6.1). Nor is it the (different) idea of substance he appeals to when he says, during this passage, that 'we have no perfect idea of substance; but . . . taking it for *something, that can exist by itself,* 'tis evident every perception is a substance, and every distinct part of a perception a distinct substance' (244/1.4.5.24). It takes practice to handle these apparent contradictions in Hume's text, but it's not that hard (see the quotation from Kant on p. 8 n. 17).

[35] For references see p. 8 n. 18.

'uniting principle among our internal perceptions', which is 'as unintelligible as that among external objects' (169/1.3.14.29).

Nor, to take a quite different example, does it have the same content as the 'useless' and 'incomprehensible' (but also 'very natural') 'fiction' in accordance with which we take ourselves to have a notion of equality that transcends possible experience (48/1.2.4.2). In this case Hume says that we're led into this 'incomprehensible' 'fiction' by 'sound reason', which 'convinces us that there are bodies *vastly* more minute than those, which appear to the senses', and so leads us to think that two figures that are equal may become unequal by subtraction of minute parts that are too small for us to notice their removal. What is said to be 'incomprehensible' or 'unintelligible' is laid out in a completely comprehensible and intelligible way, and what we learn, again, is that the terms 'incomprehensible' and 'unintelligible' mean, in effect, something like 'not justified by, not justifiably applicable on the basis of, empirical experience'. They don't mean incomprehensible or unintelligible in our sense. As this passage shows, it's not possible to read Hume correctly, when he talks of the unintelligible and the incomprehensible, unless you grant that he allows that we can have sound reason to believe something that is unintelligible and incomprehensible in his sense. Every working physicist today will agree, but we didn't have to wait for quantum mechanics to find out.[36]

Returning to the case of personal identity, it's an elementary mistake to take the sentence

It cannot . . . be from any . . . impressions . . . that the idea of self is deriv'd; and consequently there is no such idea (251/§2)

to show that Hume thinks that we have no idea of self at all. For, first, this is to fail to place the sentence in its context, i.e. within the scope of his claim, earlier in the same paragraph, that we have no 'idea of self, *after the manner it is here explain'd*', i.e. no idea of the self as something 'constant and invariable' that has 'perfect identity and simplicity'. Secondly, to say that we have no 'idea of self, after the manner it is here explain'd', isn't to say that such an idea or mental element doesn't exist. It exists all right. The philosophers Hume is criticizing—he had Samuel Clarke and Joseph

---

[36] We have 'an obscure and implicit notion of a perfect and entire equality'; 'we form the loose idea of a perfect standard to these figures, without being able to explain or comprehend it' (48–9/1.2.4.24–5).

Butler particularly in mind—are the objects of his criticism precisely because they're operating with some such idea or mental element. What's more, they believe the idea to be directly warranted in or by experience.[37] Hume's point, again, is simply that the idea, the mental element, with the content that it has, isn't warranted by experience. Here no idea = no warranted idea. The content of the idea is, otherwise, clear enough. Still unclear in some sense, no doubt, but not non-existent; and clear enough for the question of whether something exists that answers to the idea to be a real question, albeit (on the terms of 1.4.6) unanswerable, now and forever.[38]

2.5 Where is Hume?

Hume can't be an ontological bundle theorist because he's a sceptic. Two positions remain. The first is that he is, pre-Appendix, perfectly agnostic on the question of whether there's anything more to the mind than a series of experiences. The second is that he does in fact believe that there's something more to the mind, but that we can't know its nature.

Which position is Hume's? The second: 'the essence of the mind [is] unknown'. There is, however, a sense in which the first also has a place. The situation is a little delicate, dialectically speaking, in a way that is characteristic of the *Treatise* as a whole. Thus one can, perhaps, say that pre-Appendix Hume is agnostic on the question of whether there is anything more to the mind than a series of experiences. If one does this, however, one must immediately qualify one's statement by saying that he is agnostic only in the strictly negative sense that he doesn't think that one needs to appeal to anything more, in laying out a philosophy of human nature, than the bundle view of the mind. It's this view, I believe, that he so painfully renounces in the Appendix (see Part 3). He realizes that he can't effectively answer the objection that he has appealed to something more.

---

[37] See e.g. Butler: 'upon comparing the consciousnesses of one's self, or one's own existence in any two moments, there . . . immediately arises to the mind the idea of personal identity' (1736: 440).

[38] We can allow that Hume's dramatic claim that no such idea even exists is literally true in the sense that no such idea exists in properly conducted philosophy as he conceives of it.

If one allows this qualified sense in which pre-Appendix Hume is agnostic on the question of whether there is more to the mind than a series of experiences, one must then re-emphasize the point that Hume is a 'moderate' sceptic, and that as a moderate sceptic he's not in fact agnostic on the question, but rather takes it for granted that there is something more to the mind than just a series of experiences.

There's a helpful statement of the moderate sceptical position in 1.4.3 of the *Treatise*. Moderate scepticism, or 'true philosophy', agrees with common sense about things like causal power and physical objects (and minds that are more than just a series of experiences).[39] It agrees that they exist. It simply insists that we can't know their *nature*, their 'ultimate' nature. True philosophy rigorously avoids the temptation to which 'false philosophy' succumbs: the temptation of thinking it can know more about the nature of things than is given in experience. True philosophers maintain a state of true epistemic *epoche*, perfectly agnostic suspension of belief, with respect to such matters.[40] They don't, however, doubt that more *exists* than is given in experience. That doubt is immoderate, and Hume is in any case confident that he can pursue his negative, sceptical, epistemological projects, and his positive, explanatory, psychological projects, within the framework of his moderate scepticism.

In an addition to the *Treatise* first published in the Appendix, alongside his confession of the failure of his account of personal identity, and at a time when he is already much more aware of the likely misunderstandings of his position, Hume puts the point as follows, in another admirable counsel of moderation:

As long as we confine our speculations to **the appearances** of objects to our senses, without entering into disquisitions concerning *their real nature and operations*, we are safe from all difficulties, and can never be embarrass'd by any question. . . . If we carry our enquiry beyond the appearances of objects to the senses, I am afraid, that most of our conclusions will be full of scepticism and uncertainty. Thus if it be ask'd, whether or not the invisible and intangible distance [between objects] be always full of **body**, or of something that by an improvement of our organs might become visible or tangible, I must acknowledge, that I find no very decisive arguments on either side; tho' I am inclin'd to the contrary opinion, as being

---

[39] See 223–4/1.4.3.9–10, which merit careful reading.

[40] When the pressure is on, true philosophers rely on 'carelessness and inattention', 'indolence and indifference' (218/1.4.2.56, 223/1.4.3.9), words which have, here, no pejorative implication.

more suitable to vulgar and popular notions. If *the Newtonian* philosophy be rightly understood it will be found to mean no more. A vacuum is asserted: That is, bodies are said to be plac'd after such a manner, as to receive bodies betwixt them, without impulsion or penetration. *The real nature of this position of bodies is unknown.* We are only acquainted with its effects on the senses, and its power of receiving body. Nothing is more suitable to that philosophy, than a modest scepticism to a certain degree, and a fair confession of ignorance in subjects, that exceed all human capacity.[41]

2.6 Mental geography; the science of man

When we turn back to Hume's account of the mind, which is the heart of his 'science of man' (xv/Int§4), a number of further observations seem worthwhile.[42]

[1] The first and simplest is that Hume's central project is a 'mental geography, or delineation of *the distinct parts and powers of the mind*'. 'It cannot be doubted', he says, 'that *the mind is endowed with several powers and faculties,* [and] that these powers are distinct from each other'. His hope is that 'philosophy . . . may . . . discover, at least in some degree, *the secret springs and principles, by which the human mind is actuated in its operations*' (13–14/1.15). 'At least in some degree': he thinks that there is only so much that philosophy can do. For 'to me it seems evident, that the essence of the mind [is] equally unknown to us with that of external bodies'.[43]

This is very helpful, because it follows from these remarks that the mind can't be just a series of experiences, on Hume's view. For he holds that 'the

---

[41] 628–9/1.2.5.26. On the issue of the vacuum the Nortons note that Hume is 'more inclined to believe, as ordinary people do, that there are vacuums (that there are empty spaces) even though we have no idea of a vacuum' (2000: 44). They rightly attribute to him a belief about vacua while acknowledging that he takes himself to have no empirically contentful idea of a vacuum.

[42] Here I draw on Craig 1987: 111–20 and Strawson 1989: 128–31. It's striking (alarming) that some have read Hume in such a way that the first two observations have been thought to have no force.

[43] Here Hume takes up a (Newtonian) methodological position parallel to that of the early behaviourists. Just as it didn't occur to the early behaviourists to deny the existence of inner mental states of consciousness—they simply chose to restrict their experimentation to the recording and measuring of publicly observable phenomena—so too Hume doesn't deny the existence of the mind considered as something more than a series of perceptions. It's just that the essence of the mind is unknown to us and that it's 'impossible to form any notion of its powers and qualities otherwise than from careful and exact experiments, and the observation of those particular effects, which result from its different circumstances and situations' (xvii/Int§8).

[experiences] of the mind are perfectly known' (366/2.2.6.2), as remarked on page 11, and nothing can be both unknown and perfectly known. Nor can a thing have any 'secret springs and principles' that are at best partially discoverable if it's just a series of perfectly known experiences. Hume regularly makes the point that nothing is hidden, so far as experiences are concerned, noting, for example, that 'since all actions and sensations of the mind are known to us by consciousness, they must necessarily appear in every particular what they are, and be what they appear'; for 'consciousness never deceives' (190/1.4.2.7, 66/7.13). They can't, then, be all there is to the mind. There is no sense in which Hume is an ontological bundle theorist.

[2] The second observation is that Hume is deeply committed to the existence of what he calls 'the imagination'. The Imagination—the word is a term of art for Hume, and I will mark my use of it in his sense by capitalizing its first letter—is the most important single explanatory posit in his philosophy. It's central and essential to his science of human nature, and it involves far more than what we today think of as the imagination. The Imagination, he says, is 'a kind of magical faculty in the soul, which . . . is . . . inexplicable by the utmost efforts of human understanding'.[44] It's what leads us to come to believe that we have direct experience of external objects and causal power (and of a single continuing mind or self) on exposure to certain sorts of regularities in our experience, and it seems plain that its existence, and its operation in accordance with the 'unintelligible' (169/1.3.14.29) principles of the 'connexion or association of ideas' (14/1.1.5.3) that govern the way our experiences succeed each other in our minds, can't be supposed to consist merely in the existence of a collection or sequence of (perfectly known) experiences. It's something 'endow'd with . . . powers' that transposes, presents, changes, unites, distinguishes, separates, breaks up, joins, mixes and varies ideas, and can be disrupted by a 'ferment of the blood'.[45] There's a fundamental respect in which 'the memory, senses, and understanding are . . . all of them founded on the imagination, or the vivacity of our ideas' (265/1.4.7.3).

---

[44] 24/1.1.7.15. Once again, to say that a thing is unintelligible and inexplicable isn't to say that it doesn't exist. It can't be unintelligible and inexplicable unless it does exist.

[45] 95/1.3.7.3, 10/1.1.3.4, 10/1.1.4.1, 24/1.1.7.15, 42/1.2.4.17, 628/1.3.7.7, 123/1.3.10.9. Hume is by conviction a materialist, in spite of his official scepticism, and takes it the mind is wholly in the brain; see e.g. pp. 98–9 below.

Intense empiricists (i.e. non-Humean, twentieth-century empiricists) may insist that expressions like 'the imagination' or 'the memory' are to be treated as—roughly—nothing but convenient abbreviatory names for complex patterns among experiences. They may propose to treat 'the imagination' as a name for a 'fiction' in something very like Hume's sense, i.e. a mere posit or hypothesis, and take it that it's not really a power or faculty of anything at all. That's fine, so long as they don't claim that this is Hume's own view of the matter. That would be a tricky position for him to adopt, given that it is the Imagination, 'operated upon' by 'habit' and 'experience', that is, for him, the source of all 'fictions'.[46]

Points [1] and [2] pull together when Hume speaks specifically of our ignorance of the mind. The Imagination is 'inexplicable by the utmost efforts of human understanding', as just remarked. Reason is similarly puzzling: it's 'a wonderful and unintelligible instinct in our souls' (179/ 1.3.16.9) which, unintelligible as it is, nevertheless exists—although it can't possibly be a set of perfectly known experiences, or a property of such a set, or of some subset of such a set. The same goes for 'the *understanding*, that is, . . . the general and more establish'd properties of the imagination' (267/1.4.7.7). Hume explicitly identifies the understanding with the Imagination considered in a specific light: considered specifically as a faculty that operates according to 'principles which are permanent, irresistable and universal', 'solid, permanent, and consistent'; considered, that is, independently of its capacities for fantasy, daydream, storytelling, and fiction in the modern restricted sense of the word 'fiction' (225, 226/ 1.4.4.1–2). He also holds that one *reasons* on the basis of these principles of the understanding, although they are in his terminology principles of the *Imagination*, and indeed that one 'reasons justly and naturally' in accordance with them (225/1.4.4.1).

[3] These two observations prove—again—that Hume didn't think that there was nothing more to the mind than experiences or perceptions. But the point can be made with even greater force.[47] Let us call a simple

---

[46] 265/1.4.7.3; see also p. 132 below. Hume's use of the term 'fiction' is often misunderstood; for one point see Strawson (1989: 55n). Note that 'feign' and 'fiction' are English versions of the Latin verb 'fingo' which features in Newton's famous remark: 'hypotheses non fingo', i.e. 'I do not put forward hypotheses, I don't posit anything unwarranted by the empirical data'. Quine expresses the same empiricist view when he talks of the 'myth of physical objects, . . . posits comparable, epistemologically, to the gods of Homer' (1951: 44).

[47] Here I draw on Strawson 1989: 130, and put aside the case of complex ideas.

impression of Y a *Y-impression*, and a simple idea of Y a *Y-idea*. It's a central tenet of Hume's empiricism that a Y-idea can arise in my mind only if I've already had a Y-impression. His account of why this is so is well known: if a Y-idea is to occur it must be 'deriv'd from' or 'copy'd from' or 'depend' on a Y-impression.[48] And so it is, on his view: when 'an impression first strikes upon the senses', he says, 'there is a copy taken by the mind, which remains after the impression ceases; and this we call an idea' (1.1.2.1/8). But if the mind is just a bundle of distinct experiences with no hidden content (their contents are 'perfectly known'), then *there is no possible way in which this can happen*. For where does the Y-idea 'remain ... after the impression ceases'—given that I then go on to experience or think about Z, V, W, and many other things, and have no conscious thought of Y? Where can the Y-idea do its remaining, if the mind is just a bundle of distinct experiences with no hidden content?[49] How can the Y-idea be there to be triggered a year later—say by an X-impression? (Suppose I had a whole flurry of X-impressions followed by Y-impressions when I first had an impression of Y, and then had no X-impressions for a year, and then had an X-impression or X-idea, which gave rise to a Y-idea.) On the bundle view, the Y-idea no longer has any sort of existence when I've gone on to Z, V, W, and so on, and have no conscious thought of Y. For all experiences or perceptions are conscious occurrences.

If the bundle view of the mind is the right one, then, there is no possible structure or mechanism given which the occurrence of the original Y-impression or Y-idea can be the basis of the occurrence of any later, temporally non-contiguous Y-idea. The whole phenomenon of memory, furthermore, must be a complete illusion.

—This point has no force. Your argument not only depends on the view that the outright ontological regularity theory of causation is untenable; it also depends on the view that the outright ontological regularity theory is wrongly attributed to Hume. Both these views will be disputed by those who think Hume adopts an outright ontological bundle theory of mind.

---

[48] 4/1.1.1.8, 10/1.1.3.4. I'll stick to simple ideas, but in the case of a complex idea Y, composed of simple ideas Z, V, and W, say, the claim is that Y can arise in the mind only if Z, V, and W have previously arisen.

[49] The 'where' is metaphorical in as much as it is not restricted to space. Note that it would be a simple mistake to think that Hume's claim that many perceptions exist 'no where' (235–6/1.4.5.10) provides materials for a response to this point. (Those tempted by this move may re-run the point for the restricted case of the 'perceptions ... of the sight and feeling' (236/1.4.5.10)). For some further discussion of perceptions that exist 'no where' see 3.7 below.

The outright ontological regularity theory of causation is very silly,[50] and I know of no evidence that it ever even occurred to Hume, as remarked on pages 27–8. One can, however, put this to one side, for the force of point [3] is effectively unchanged even when one supposes that Hume did hold such a view. For if we suppose, with the bundle theory, that the mind is really nothing but a series of ontologically distinct experiences, we again face the difficulty that there can be no causal relation, no dependence relation, between the first Y-impression and any later Y-idea that is not its immediate successor in the series of experiences, or between the first Y-idea and any later Y-idea that is not its immediate successor. For in this case the temporal contiguity condition on causal relations that is laid down by the regularity theory of causation fails to hold. If an X-impression occurs at some later date, and is followed by a Y-idea, and even if this always happens, the occurrence of the Y-idea can have nothing to do with any earlier Y-impression or original Y-idea. The earlier Y-impression can't be its cause or origin or source, or something it depends on. The Y-idea in the mind must in each case spring from nowhere, or be caused by the X-impression alone without there being any question of its having any other source or origin or basis. For there is absolutely nothing more to the mind than a series of occurrent experiences, on the outright ontological bundle view.

Plainly, then, there must be something more to the mind than just the occurrent series of conscious experiences, on Hume's view—even if he espouses the outright ontological regularity theory of causation, which he doesn't. There must be something more to the mind if there's to be any sense in which ideas derive from, or are copies of, or depend on, impressions they don't immediately succeed. There must be something—however unknown or unintelligible to us—that *serves to preserve contents through time*, so that a Y-impression (or first Y-idea) occurring at a given time can serve as the basis of the occurrence of a Y-idea at some temporally non-contiguous later time. Remarks like 'frequent repetition of any idea infixes it in the imagination' (116/1.3.9.17), which directly address the issue of how contents are preserved through time, are radically incompatible with a picture of the mind as nothing more than a series of ontologically distinct (conscious) experiences. Hume certainly holds that experiences are

[50] It's silly in every sense, including Broad's sense (1925: 5) and Eddington's sense (1928: 260).

all we have so far as we have a clear, philosophically legitimate, empirically warranted idea of the mind suitable for use in knowledge claims about the nature of the mind (rather than merely about its existence). But he doesn't and can't hold that that is all there is to the mind. Nor does he. 'The essence of the mind . . . is unknown to us'. This is not the claim that there might in fact be nothing more to the mind than a series of perceptions (in which case the essence of the mind would be fully known after all), but that we can't know whether this is so or not. It's the claim that there is definitely more, but we don't know its fundamental or essential nature.

Consider the case (so central for Hume) in which an impression of A immediately gives rise to an idea of B. Why does this happen? Because one has often seen As followed by Bs in the past. But the experiences or perceptions one has had in the ten seconds preceding this impression of an A have—we may suppose—been only of Cs, Ds, and Es. One hasn't seen or thought of As or Bs for at least ten seconds (or ten minutes, or ten years). How, then, can a B-idea be ready to arise in this way when, and because, one has an A-impression? How can anything that has happened in the temporally non-contiguous past possibly be of any relevance at all if [i] there really is nothing more to a mind than just a series of ontologically entirely distinct fleeting experiences with no 'real connexion' between them, and [ii] the whole existence or being of that mind in the last ten seconds or so has been a matter of the existence of experiences of Cs, Ds, and Es and absolutely nothing more?

Parallel points can be made about memory, as remarked. Those who think that Hume is a bundle theorist will have to go all the way. Dismissing his statement that the essence of the mind is unknown, and his cautious hope that philosophy may none the less be able to 'discover, at least in some degree, the secret springs and principles, by which the human mind is actuated in its operations' (14/1.15), they'll have to say that Hume doesn't really think this at all—that in fact he holds that all aspects of the mind lie wholly open to inspection. It's true that he says that all we can know of the mind are experiences and the sequential patterns they form, but on the outright ontological interpretation this isn't an admission of ignorance. For according to this interpretation, experiences and their patterns are all that exist, metaphysically speaking, so far as the mind is concerned, and they're 'perfectly known'. So if Hume is an ontological bundle theorist he must think that we can discover 'the ultimate original qualities of human nature' after all, at least so far as the mind is concerned. But he is quite clear that we can't.

Standing back, we have two views of Hume on the mind: Hume the perfect agnostic and Hume the moderate sceptic. The second view is central, but we can perhaps allow that the first—which differs from the latter in that it involves suspension of belief not just about the nature of the something-more-than-experiences but also about its very existence—is also in play. I think, though, that it's in play only in the strictly negative sense given earlier. It's in play only in so far as Hume takes it, pre-Appendix, that he can when operating strictly inside his empiricist framework carry through all his philosophical purposes without having to appeal essentially to knowledge of anything more than his empiricism can warrant; which is, in the case of the mind, just a bundle of experiences.

2.7 Mind and cause: a comparison

I'm preparing to enter the central textual shrine of Hume on personal identity, but I want to stop for a moment and appose two sets of quotations. First, the quotations given on page 47, according to which minds or selves or persons or thinking beings are

'nothing but a bundle or collection of different perceptions'; 'they are the successive perceptions only, that constitute the mind'; a 'chain of causes and effects . . . constitute[s] our self or person'; a 'composition of . . . perceptions . . . forms the self'; a 'train . . . of perceptions . . . compose a mind'; a 'succession of perceptions . . . constitutes [a] mind or thinking principle [or] self or person'; 'what we call a mind, is nothing but a heap or collection of different perceptions, united together by certain relations'; a 'connected mass of perceptions . . . constitute[s] a thinking being'; 'a connected heap of perceptions'; a 'succession of perceptions . . . constitutes our self or person'. 'It must be our several particular perceptions, that compose the mind. I say, compose the mind, not belong to it.'

In apposition, a group of quotations from Hume's discussion of causation in 1.3.14:

'this multiplicity of resembling instances . . . constitutes the very essence of power or connexion'; 'necessity . . . is nothing but an internal impression of the mind'; 'The necessary connexion betwixt causes and effects *is* the [inferential] transition arising from the accustom'd union'; the 'propensity . . . to pass from an object to the idea of its usual attendant . . . is the essence of necessity. . . . Upon the whole, necessity is something, that exists in the mind, not in objects. . . . Either we have no idea of necessity, or necessity is nothing but that determination of the thought to pass from causes to effects and from effects to causes'; 'the necessity or power, which unites causes and effects, lies in the determination of the mind to pass from the one to the other. . . . The efficacy or energy of causes . . . belongs entirely to the soul, which considers the union of two or more objects in all past instances. . . .' 'Tis here that the real power of causes is plac'd, along with their connexion and necessity'; the 'customary transition is, therefore, the same with the power and necessity'; 'this determination of the mind forms the necessary connexion of these objects'; it is 'the constant conjunction of objects, along with the determination of the mind, which constitutes a physical necessity'. (163–71/1.3.14.16–33)

As regards the first group of quotations, we know that Hume doesn't think that this is all there is to the mind. The quotations give all the empirically acceptable content of the idea of the mind, but 'the essence of the mind is unknown'. As regards the second group of quotations, it's no less clear, except to those for whom the contrary notion is riveted in the mind, that Hume doesn't think that this is all there is to power or efficacy in 'external bodies'. The quotations give all the empirically acceptable content of the idea of power or efficacy or 'necessary connexion', but 'the essence of . . . external bodies', including of course their 'ultimate and operating principle' (267/1.4.7.5), is 'equally unknown to us with that' of the mind.

One should not think that the question of the essence of external bodies is separate from the question of their operating principle, their 'internal structure or operating principle' (169/1.3.14.29), their 'power or operating principle' (159/1.3.14.7). These are terms for aspects of the essence of external bodies. Hume goes on to observe that most philosophers agree that 'the ultimate force and efficacy of nature is perfectly unknown to us, and that 'tis in vain we search for it in all the known qualities of matter' (159/1.3.14.8), and this prompts him to comment on the Cartesians, who precisely deny that 'the essence of . . . external bodies [is] unknown to us':

the *Cartesians* . . . , having establish'd it as a principle, that we are perfectly acquainted with the essence of matter, have very naturally inferr'd, that it is endow'd with no efficacy, and that 'tis impossible for it of itself to communicate motion, or produce any of those effects, which we ascribe to it. As the essence of matter consists in extension [on their view], and as extension implies not actual motion, but only mobility; they conclude, that the energy, which produces the motion, cannot lie in the extension. (159/1.3.14.8)

Their move is illegitimate, on Hume's view, for the essence of external bodies is unknown to us. No one should claim to know that matter is—

that external bodies are—'endow'd with no efficacy'. In fact our only clear and empirically contentful notion of efficacy derives from a subjective feeling; so it can't possibly apply to external bodies. So although we do know that external objects stand in relations of *existential dependence*—we know that 'the existence of one is dependent on that of the other' (212/ 1.4.2.47)—we have no empirically contentful conception of what this 'real connexion' amounts to. But we certainly shouldn't say that there is no such thing.[51]

There is, then, a striking parallel between Hume's claims about the empirically contentful idea of the mind and his claims about the empirically contentful idea of the power or efficacy. Both employ forms of words that move from 'this is all we know' to 'this is all there is' in a potentially misleading way. A crucial disanalogy remains, in that Hume's overall theory doesn't commit him to assuming more about external bodies and their efficacy than his empiricism allows, whereas it may commit him to assuming more about the mind than his empiricism allows. This is the subject of Part 3.

2.8 Three theses

There are still a number of things to do before considering the famous opening of 'Of personal identity'. I want next to list three theses that Hume accepts and that it helps to bear in mind.

[1] The first, already mentioned, is the *Experience/Experiencer* thesis, the thesis that

an experience entails an experiencer, a subject of experience,

which Hume rightly never questions (2.3, p. 40).

An experience also necessarily involves a content, an experiential content; this is another necessary truth. Using 'E' for 'experience', 'S' for 'subject of experience', and 'C' for '(mental or experiential) content',[52] one can represent these two truths as follows

---

[51] These points, together with those in 1.4 and 2.4, refute Millican's recent 'decisive objection' to the view that Hume is a sceptical realist about causation (Millican 2010a; see also Millican 2007a, 2007b, 2009, 2010b). I return briefly to the question on pp. 110–11 below.

[52] This is occurrent experiential content understood in the natural, traditional, Humean, 'internalist' way, which takes it that a veridical experience of a tree and a qualitatively identical

$[E \rightarrow [S \& C]].$

Whatever else an experience is, it necessarily involves a subject and a content—whatever the relation between them and whatever else they are. One might call this the *Experience/Subject/Content* thesis: the *ESC* thesis for short. Later on I will question whether this is really the best way to represent it.[53]

It may be said that appeal to the Experience/Experiencer thesis begs the question when the question is whether Hume did entertain the possibility of a 'no owner' view of experiences. But this question should be begged if not begging it means accepting that it's a real possibility that Hume held the view that an experience can exist without an experiencer—without even an experiencer that lasts as long as the experience! (I'll return to this point.)

A second reply is more conciliatory. There's a version of the no-ownership thesis that is compatible with the Experience/Experiencer thesis, on one assumption, and it's something that the *Treatise* does indeed register as a possibility. For Hume does hold that [i] we have no good empirical grounds for thinking that there is a self or subject or 'owner' of experience that lasts longer than an experience. So if one assumes that [ii] anything that can qualify as a self or subject or 'owner' of experience *must* be something that has some sort of longer-term existence, then one can after all take Hume to be arguing that [iii] we have no grounds for thinking that experiences have a self or subject or 'owner' of experience. Now it was assumed in Hume's time (as remarked on p. 42), and is often assumed today, that [iv] anything that can qualify as a subject or 'owner' of experience must be something that has some sort of longer-term existence, and relative to that assumption Hume is indeed expounding [v] a 'no owner' view—but without in any way questioning the Experience/Experiencer thesis.

[2] The second thesis, also noted earlier (p. 41), is the *Cartesian Certainty* thesis that

---

hallucination of a tree have the same content. (An 'externalist' conception of mental content or 'representational' content holds that the content of my mental state when I'm looking at a tree isn't anything mental but is the tree itself. In this case the veridical and hallucinatory experiences don't have the same content.)

[53]   The fact that the S and the C must be the S and the C *of* E is assumed, and isn't explicitly represented in the formula.

one can know that one exists in the present moment of experience, even if there is much one can't know about what sort of thing one is, and even if one can't know whether one endures beyond the present moment of experience.

This claim, routine at the time, and surely correct, is central to Hume's discussion of personal identity, and it recurs when he's summing up his overall sceptical predicament in the next section of the *Treatise*. When we put on the sceptical pressure, we're driven into the position which is sometimes called 'solipsism of the present moment', in which only our own existence is beyond doubt, along with that of our present experience. The question that arises at the furthest point of sceptical doubt is 'Where am I, or what? From what causes do I derive my existence, and to what condition shall I return?' (268–9/1.4.7.6). I exist, all right, and so do my experiences, but when it comes to our experiences, we can strictly speaking admit to exist 'only those [experiences], which are immediately present to our consciousness'.[54]

[3] The third thesis is the *Intimate Idea* thesis, the thesis that

the idea, or rather impression of ourselves is always intimately present with us, and that our consciousness gives us so lively a conception of our own person, that 'tis not possible to imagine, that any thing can in this particular go beyond it.[55]

Given that 'when Hume uses the term "self" or "person", he generally means to be referring only to the mind',[56] and given that he holds that 'consciousness never deceives' (66/7.13), this endorsement of the Intimate Idea thesis in Book 2 of the *Treatise* appears to suffice on its own to show that Hume has no thought of claiming that there is no sort of impression or idea of self at all, rather than claiming simply that there is (for example) no idea or impression of an uninterrupted, perfectly simple and continuing self.

—You can't appeal to Hume's endorsement of the Intimate Idea thesis when considering his views on personal identity, because it occurs in his discussion of the

[54] 265/1.4.7.3. See Descartes's *Second Meditation*: one can't infer *anything* about the ultimate substantial nature of oneself (the subject of experience) from the mere fact that one exists and knows that one does: 'I know that I exist; the question is, what is this "I" that I know?', Descartes asks. 'I do not know', he replies; but whatever I suppose, and whatever the truth is, 'for all that I am still something' (1641: 18).

[55] 317/2.1.11.4; see also 320/2.1.11.8: 'ourself is always intimately present to us'; also 339–40/2.2.2.15–16, 354/2.2.4.7, 427/2.3.7.1.

[56] Pike 1967: 161; see 2.1 above. See also Penelhum 1955, Biro 1993: 47–8. Note that there are references to 'self' or 'person' in Books 2 and 3 of the *Treatise* that don't have a purely or even primarily mental reference (see e.g. 298/2.1.8.1, 303/2.1.9.1, 329/2.2.1.2).

passions in Book 2 of the *Treatise*, and he explicitly distinguishes between 'personal identity, as it regards our thought or imagination, and as it regards our passions or the concern we take in ourselves' (253/§5). Furthermore, Book 2's apparent endorsement of the Intimate Idea thesis is incompatible with the observation in Book I that the 'ideas of self and person are never very fix'd nor determinate . . . in common life'. (189–90/1.4.2.6)

As to the first point, few, perhaps, will doubt that appeal to the Intimate Idea thesis is legitimate in the present context. There is, however, no need to argue the point, for it plays no essential or indeed significant part in what follows.

As to the second point, the 'liveliness' of the idea of the self that is in question in the discussion of the passions in Book 2 is principally a matter of emotional charge and practical weight. But even if we suppose that it has great force and vivacity independently of these things, it seems that an idea can have great liveliness without being fixed and determinate.[57] Similarly for 'intimate presence'. There's no tension between the claim that the idea or impression of self is intimately present and the claim that it isn't fixed or determinate. This in fact is very much how it is with us— Hume's phenomenological description is as usual extremely accurate. The idea or experience of self is experienced as both intimately present and as very hard to fix on or pin down. John Updike makes a very good point when he observes that our names 'are used for convenience by others but figure marginally in our own minds, which know ourselves as an entity too vast and vague to name'.[58]

2.9 Berkeley's bundle

The last thing I want to do before considering Hume's intimate entry into himself is to record some complexities in the bundle view as he presents it. Those who wish can skip to the summary of these complexities in 2.13.

It's useful to begin by considering the bundle view as set out by Berkeley in the notebooks he kept before writing the *Principles* and the *Dialogues*; in which (substituting 'experience' for 'perception' and 'perceive') five consecutive entries read as follows:

---

[57] See Biro 1993: 62n. 19.
[58] 2000: 76. Compare Woolf 1931, *passim*.

577 The very existence of ideas constitutes the soul.

578 Consciousness, [experiences], existence of ideas seem to be all one.

579 Consult, ransack your understanding; what find you there besides several [experiences] or thoughts. What mean you by the word 'mind'? You must mean something that you [experience] . . . .

580 Mind is a congeries of [experiences]. Take away [experiences] and you take away the mind; put the [experiences] and you put the mind.

581 Say you the mind is not the [experiences], but that thing which [experiences]? I answer you are abus'd by the words 'that' and 'thing'; these are vague empty words without a meaning.[59]

Berkeley records this view in his notebooks because it's a view that a radical empiricist programme pushes one towards, but he rejects it categorically in his published work. He acknowledges that one can have no *idea* of the mind or soul, considered as something distinct from experiences, on his meaning-empiricist principles ('What mean you by the word 'mind'? You must mean something that you perceive'), but he doesn't waver from the view that one can none the less have a *notion* of the mind or soul, and can know both that it exists and that it is distinct from its experiences. When Hylas charges Berkeley's spokesman Philonous with adherence to a bundle theory in the 'Third Dialogue', saying

in consequence of your own principles, it should follow that you are only a system of floating ideas, without any substance to support them,

Philonous replies

How often must I repeat that I know or am conscious of my own being; and that I myself am not my ideas, but somewhat else, a thinking active principle that perceives, knows, wills, and operates about them (1713: 198)

and in the *Principles* Berkeley writes as follows:

besides all [the] endless variety of ideas . . . there is . . . something which knows or perceives them, and exercises divers operations . . . about them. This perceiving acting being is what I call *mind*, *spirit*, *soul*, or *myself*. By which words I do not denote any one of my ideas, but a thing entirely distinct from them, wherein they exist. . . . (1710: §2)

Berkeley, then, is no bundle theorist. It's worth recording the view he set out in his notebooks because it was in the air.

---

[59] Berkeley 1707–8: 307. I've added quotation marks where words are mentioned rather than used, put in some punctuation, and spelt out abbreviations.

2.10 The Simple Fiction view

Hume spends much of 'Of personal identity' explaining how we come to believe in the existence of a self that is

[+A]   something that has long-term existence
[+B]   a diachronically simple or single (non-compound) thing
[+C]   a diachronically continuous thing,

whether or not we also come to believe—either naturally, or because we have some religious or philosophical agenda—that the self is

[+D]   a diachronically unchanging thing[60]
[+E]   a synchronically simple (or non-compound) thing.

His account of how this happens is in key respects the same as the account he gives of how we come to believe in continuing physical objects like tables and chairs. It involves a 'feigning' or 'fiction', a supposition or posit or hypothesis that comes naturally—inevitably—to all normal human beings and is a result of the action of the Imagination. We naturally posit, and then naturally come to believe in, a continuing entity, although belief in its existence isn't warranted by the empirical evidence. In the particular case of the mind or self or thinking principle we posit a [+A] persisting thing that is [+B] diachronically non-compound and [+C] diachronically continuous, on exposure to a series of (necessarily subject-involving) experiences that are, considered individually, fleeting [−A], and, considered collectively, diachronically multiple [−B] and diachronically discontinuous [−C].

   [+A], [+B], and [+C], with or without [+D] and [+E], constitute what one might call the 'simple' version of the fiction view—the *Simple Fiction* view, for short.

2.11 The Vegetable Fiction view

There is, however, a complication. For Hume doesn't think that a persisting self, considered as a posit or fiction that we come to believe in, is a posit of quite the same sort as a table or stone. He thinks, following Locke, that

---

[60] Diachronically unchanging in respect of its substance: even advocates of the immaterial soul allow that (human) selves change over time in respect of their mental contents.

it's more like the posit of a persisting plant or vegetable (see e.g. 255/§6, 259/§15). Here a number of ideas are densely concertinaed together, but all that one needs to bring out, I think, is the following. Consider a stone. In the standard case, according to Hume, we're led to believe in the existence of a single continuing stone as a result of the fact that [+1] we have a series of strongly qualitatively resembling experiences.[61] We also take it that [+2] (= [+B]) the stone consists of the same material parts or particles over time, and that [+3] the stone does in fact remain very similar in overall character and hence appearance—this being, indeed, the explanation, in the common-sense scheme, of the fact that [+4] the stone gives rise to a series of strongly (qualitatively) resembling experiences over time.[62]

Plants are quite different. For, first, we can be led to believe in the existence of a single continuing plant by a series of experiences that is far more various over time than the series of experiences that leads us to believe in the existence of a stone [−1]. Secondly, we take a plant to be the same thing over time even if we know it to be constituted by a succession of different parts or particles [−2], and we take it to be the same thing over time even if it changes greatly in overall character and appearance over time [−3], and ('therefore', in the common-sense scheme) gives rise to strikingly different experiences over time [−4].

The case of the mind or self is much more like the case of the plant than the stone, according to Hume. For, first, the series of experiences that leads us to believe in the existence of a single continuing mind or self is often highly various in character [−1].[63] Secondly, we take a mind or self to be the same thing over time even if this involves taking it to be something that changes greatly in overall character and appearance over time, given development of personality, accumulation of memories, and so on, in addition to constantly changing occurrent contents [−3]. As Hume says, we normally allow that 'the same person may vary his character and

---

[61] Hume's principal account of this is in 200–04/1.4.2.29–34, or more widely 194–209/ 1.4.2.18–42.

[62] This is compressed—I'm ignoring qualitative differences arising from (for example) different visual perspectives. For a further (wholly tractable) complication, see Hume's discussion of the fire in the grate (195/1.4.2.19–20) and his use there of the notion of the 'coherence' of the experiences.

[63] 'Our thought is . . . in a perpetual flux' in which different experiences 'succeed each other with an inconceivable rapidity' (252/§4). Marcus Aurelius says that 'the mind is a whirl' (c.170: 2.14).

disposition, as well as his impressions and ideas, without losing his identity' (261/§19). Thirdly, we take the experiences that lead us to believe in the existence of a continuing mind or self to be the contents of the consciousness of the very continuing thing we are led to believe in. So in so far as we take the passing, changing experiences to be part of the very being of the thing we are led to believe in, as Hume does, they're comparable to the particles that we suppose to constitute a single plant persisting over time [−2].[64]

Here, then, we have the *Organic* or *Vegetable Fiction* view of the mind or self, according to which 'the identity, which we ascribe to the mind of man, is . . . of a like kind with that which we ascribe to vegetables and animal bodies'.[65] According to the Vegetable Fiction view, the mind or self is a diachronically compound entity, so far as its substantial composition is concerned [−B], because it consists of a succession of different (possibly temporally overlapping) parts, although it's a single diachronically continuous persisting entity in every sense in which a plant is [+A, +C]. It's also a diachronically changing entity so far as its substantial composition is concerned [−D]. It's not just its states that change; its substance changes through the 'incessant changes of its parts',[66] although it remains the same thing through time in every sense in which a plant does. It is, then, something that genuinely persists, but only in an 'organic' fashion.

If we call this form of persistence [+A^O], 'O' for 'organic', we may state the Vegetable Fiction view as follows. A self is

[+A^O]   a thing that has 'organic' long-term existence
[−B]   a diachronically compound thing
[+C]   a diachronically continuous thing
[−D]   a diachronically changing thing,

whether or not it is

[+E]   synchronically non-compound.[67]

---

[64] Again I'm passing over various complications. Here the proposed comparison is between directly experienced change (of experiences and their content) and theoretically posited change (of material particles constitutive of a material thing).

[65] 259/§15. Compare Locke 1689–1700: 2.27.6. From one perspective this is a pretty robust notion of diachronic identity—once we have 'taken the existence of body for granted in all our reasonings', as Hume says we must (187/1.4.2.1).

[66] 261/§19; here Hume is comparing the mind or soul to a republic or commonwealth made up successively of different people.

[67] I'll omit [E] from now on, as nothing much hangs on it.

2.12 The Outright Bundle view

Hume's principal aim in 'Of personal identity' is, as remarked, to give a psychological explanation of how it is that we come to believe in a continuing single self in the way that we do, given that the mind or self 'as far as we can conceive it', i.e. the mind or self as far as we have any distinct, empirically warranted, philosophically legitimate idea of it, 'is nothing but a system or train of different [experiences]' (657/Abs§28). The *Outright Bundle* view of the self—according to which selves or minds are 'nothing but a bundle or collection of different [experiences]'; according to which a 'succession of [experiences] . . . *constitutes* [a person's] mind or thinking principle', a 'composition of . . . [experiences] . . . forms the self', a 'train . . . of [experiences] . . . compose a mind' (252/§4, 260/§18, 634/App§15, 635/App§20)—simply takes the content of the empirically warranted idea of the self and treats it in an unequivocally ontological, profoundly non-Humean fashion as a description of an actually existing entity. It states accordingly that the self, in so far as there is such a thing, is

[+A]   a thing that has long-term existence
[−B]   a diachronically compound thing
[−C]   a diachronically discontinuous thing
[−D]   a diachronically changing thing.

It should be said, though, that [+A] is there only because Hume accepts as common ground, for purposes of discussion, the assumption that an account of the self or mind must be an account of something that has some sort of long-term persistence. In this sense the Outright Bundle view is conditional in form: *given* [+A], given that there must be some sort of persisting self or mind if there is to be said to be a self or mind at all, given that this is the notion whose philosophically warranted, empirically clear and distinct content is being sought, all you can really have is a [−B, −C, −D] bundle self or mind. But a bundle isn't really a single thing, a substantial unity, a continuing thing, at all. It's a bundle of such things, at best, and in this sense one might best represent the Outright Bundle view as involving [−A].

It's worth noting that outright bundle theorists don't have to accept [−C]. For although Hume's version of the bundle view seems to incorporate a straightforward non-continuity view—

when my [experiences] are remov'd for any time, as by sound sleep; so long am I insensible of myself, and may truly be said not to exist (252/§3)

—bundle theorists can coherently deny that there is ever any break in the flow of experiences that constitute a mind or self or person, for they can deny that there is a complete cessation of experience even in what we take to be dreamless sleep.[68] They may also point out that Hume's apparently clear acceptance of non-continuity is what it seems only if he also accepts the existence of objective time relative to which a bundle self constituted by a seemingly temporally gappy bundle of experiences can be said to be objectively temporally gappy.[69]

Here I'll take it that he does accept this. Even if bundle theorists aren't committed to the diachronic discontinuity of the self, nearly all versions of the bundle view incorporate this idea, and I'll take it for granted that the Outright Bundle view does, holding that a self is an entity with a *gappy* kind of long-term existence. One might call this $[+A^G]$, 'G' for 'gappy'. A self, then, is

$[+A^G]$ a thing that has (gappy) long-term existence
$[-B]$ diachronically compound
$[-C]$ diachronically discontinuous
$[-D]$ diachronically changing.

The various views discussed so far can be summarized in the following chart bearing in mind, as before, that the $[+A]$ under the Outright Bundle view could be instructively replaced by $[-A]$, a self then being something that

Outright Bundle	Simple Fiction	Vegetable Fiction
$[+A^G]$	$[+A]$	$[+A^O]$
$[-B]$	$[+B]$	$[-B]$
$[-C]$	$[+C]$	$[+C]$
$[-D]$	$[+D]$	$[-D]$

[68] It's an unsettled empirical question whether there are periods of total experiencelessness in the life of a normal human being.

[69] This is worth mentioning because some empiricists may not admit objective time in this sense. They may hold that the apparently real time frame of the world of table and chairs of our everyday experience is a posit or 'fiction', and that even if time is real, in some sense, there is (and can be) no evidence that there are real temporal gaps between successive experiences that appear to be discontinuous. (For an account of how one might dispute the existence of objective time on empiricist grounds see Foster 1982.) Such apparently discontinuous successive experiences could be distinct from each other—could be different experiences—while being continuous in the sense of having no temporal gaps between them, just as chromatically distinct coloured lines may be joined seamlessly together to form a compound but spatially continuous line.

does not really have long-term existence at all, being, precisely, a temporally discontinuous bundle of items.

2.13 Where is Hume?

Where is Hume in all this? Well, the Outright Bundle view of the self or mind is Hume's account, couched in outright ontological terms, of the character and content of the information about the self or mind that is given to us in experience. To put it in other words: it's Hume's empiricist account, couched in outright ontological terms, of the basic character of the experience on the basis of which we come to believe in the existence of the self or mind. In other words again, it's Hume's account, couched in outright ontological terms, of the distinct or philosophically legitimate positively descriptive content of our concept of the self or mind according to his empiricist theory of meaning.

The relation between the Outright Bundle view and the Fiction views, in Hume's scheme, is as follows. We find we believe in a certain entity, the self or mind, and believe it to have certain properties, as variously set out in the description of the two Fiction views above. We firmly believe that it has some sort of long-term existence, for example. And whether or not we believe it lasts for life (and perhaps beyond), we certainly believe that it's something that lasts longer than the time of a single experience. This being so, our next task as philosophers is to consider the *evidence* for the existence of such a thing. When we do so, it turns out that all we have direct experiential evidence for, so far as a subject of experience that is being assumed to last longer than the time of a single experience is concerned, is an entity that is discontinuous; compound in a strong sense (it's diachronically compound in respect of its putative substantial composition, being composed of a series of ontologically entirely distinct experiences); and changeful in an equally strong sense. And yet we believe in (or, as errant philosophers, posit or hypothesize) something quite different, something that is continuous in its existence; that isn't gappy in any sense; that isn't compound in the strong sense just mentioned; and that doesn't change so far as its basic substantial identity is concerned, even though its states change regularly.

This is the epistemological, psychological situation, according to Hume. He certainly doesn't endorse the Outright Bundle view, in spite of his abbreviatory ontologizing idiom. He is, after all, a sceptic who (perceptions apart) doesn't claim to know the final truth about how things are metaphysically, either in general or in the case of the mind: 'the essence of the mind is . . . unknown'.[70] He is, furthermore, a moderate sceptic, a sceptic who doesn't for a moment doubt (and unequivocally asserts) that there is in fact more to the mind than we know, while at the same time insisting that true philosophy—philosophy committed to operating only with clear and distinct ideas whose content is derived from experience— can and indeed must maintain a perfect agnosticism about its nature. As far as philosophy is concerned, he thinks 'the true idea of the human mind is to consider it as a system of different [experiences] or different existences' (261/ §19). What strikes him so forcefully after he's published Book 1, and leads to his confession of failure in the Appendix, or so I believe, is his realization that he can't satisfactorily answer the objection that he has within his own philosophy presupposed an idea of the mind that not only exceeds the 'true' idea of the mind, but does so in a manner that means that it can be correctly metaphysically characterized in a way that has the following unacceptable property: [a] it ascribes content to the idea of the mind that goes beyond what his empiricist theory of meaning allows; [b] this extra content can't be dismissed with handwaving about the 'wonderful', 'un-known essence' of the mind; [c] this is the case even though this kind of handwaving is sometimes entirely legitimate, given Hume's project.

We must, however, consider 'Of personal identity' further, before considering its repudiation in the Appendix.

2.14 'When I enter most intimately into what I call *myself*' 1

When I enter most intimately into what I call *myself* I always stumble on some particular [experience] or other. . . . I never can catch *myself* at any time without [an experience], and never can observe anything but [the experience].[71]

---

[70]   The point that he doesn't endorse the ontological bundle view holds even when we put aside all bundle-theory-incompatible remarks of the following kind in Books 2 and 3 of the *Treatise*: 'nature has given to the organs of the human mind, a certain disposition fitted to produce a peculiar impression or emotion, which we call *pride*' (287/2.1.5.6); 'the mind . . . has certain organs naturally fitted to produce a passion; that passion, when produc'd, naturally turns the view to a certain object' (396/2.2.11.6).

[71]   252/§3 with 'experience' substituted for 'perception'; as before, 'myself' means myself considered as a mental phenomenon.

This is the famous passage, with 'experience' substituted for 'perception' in an attempt to suspend the standard interpretative reflexes, which seem to have sunk into the words of the text in such a way that there's no clear access to the original (restore 'perception' if you prefer). Here it is again, with 'episode of experience' substituted for 'perception':

When I enter most intimately into what I call *myself* I always stumble on some particular [episode of experience] or other.... I never can catch *myself* at any time without [an episode of experience], and never can observe anything but the [episode of experience].

What does this say? It says that when I reflect in this way, two things are true. First,

[1] when I consider myself in my mental being I never catch myself without an experience.

Secondly,

[2] when I consider myself in my mental being I never observe anything but the experience—the experiencing, the episode of experience.

These two claims are linked but different. According to [1], I never get a *bare view* of the self or subject of experience. That is, I never get a view of the subject alone. I do of course always catch myself, the subject of experience that I then am, when I enter most intimately into what I call myself and observe an experience, for an experience always and necessarily involves a subject of experience.[72] But I never catch myself at any time pure, 'without an experience'.[73] Nor, therefore, and importantly, given the contemporary debate, do I catch anything that presents itself as capable of existing apart from the experience in such a way as to qualify for the title 'substance' as traditionally understood.[74]

According to [2], when I catch myself I never observe anything but the experience—the experience-event, the perception-event, the episode of experience or perceiving. The experience-event is, to be sure, an

---

[72] Hume is not here concerned with the idea that apprehending an experience requires a further distinct experience that must, as such, have a different subject from the experience apprehended.

[73] Compare Kant (1781/7: B406): 'I do not know myself through being conscious of myself as thinking, but only when I am conscious of the intuition of myself as determined with respect to the function of thought.'

[74] According to one central traditional metaphysical definition, a substance is something that can exist by itself without dependence on any other created or contingently existing thing.

experienc*ing*, a perceiv*ing*. It is a necessarily subject-involving thing. So I do indeed catch myself, the self or person or subject at that moment, in catching the experience.[75] But no self or subject presents as something distinct from the overall experience-event, as the philosophical tradition of Hume's time uniformly supposes the self or subject (or soul) to be. There's no impression of any such thing. Nothing presents as a subject that is distinct or distinguishable from the episode of experience in such a way that it can be supposed to be ontologically separate from the episode of experience, according to Hume's fundamental Separability Principle.[76] One might put the point by saying that for any given experience or set of experiences E, when E is strictly examined, no subject presents as 'E-transcendent'.

This is, I believe, absolutely correct, as a report of ordinary 'intimate entrance'. The phenomenological facts are waiting for anyone to discover.[77] The point is commonplace in the Phenomenological tradition of philosophy, and William James proposes that 'the passing Thought itself is the only *verifiable* thinker'.[78] Note, though, that Hume is not merely claiming that the subject's experience of itself in ordinary everyday experience is 'non-egological', in Sartre's terms, and neither features the subject as something distinct from the experience, nor as something enduring. He's pointing out that this is true even when one engages in some special, focused, explicit act of 'real-time' or 'live' mental self-examination, examination of one's mental goings-on as one finds them in the present moment.[79]

I'll develop this point soon. For now, one might re-express [1] symbolically by saying that I get no view with just the content

{S}

where 'S' stands as before for self or subject of experience, and the curly brackets indicate what I'll call a *phenomenological content*. I get no view of a

---

[75] I suspect that the main difficulty of convincing analytic philosophers lies in this point, given the existing tradition of Hume commentary. That said, it is thoroughly consonant with Chisholm 1969. See also the quotations from Russell and Foster on pp. 93–94 below.

[76] 'Whatever is distinct, is distinguishable; and whatever is distinguishable, is separable by the thought or imagination . . . and may be conceiv'd as separately existent, and may exist separately, without any contradiction or absurdity' (634/App§12). On this question see Garrett 1997: ch. 3.

[77] Berkeley encountered them, Priestley and Kant re-expressed them.

[78] 1890: 1.346, ch 10 *passim*. James uses the word 'thought' in Descartes's entirely general sense.

[79] I'll avoid the word 'introspect', for the most part.

subject alone at all, let alone a view of some continuing unchanging subject alone. All views of the subject are views of the subject with, involved in, an (episode of) experience. That is, they are at least of the form

$$\{S + E\},$$

where 'E' stands as before for experience. But they're not really of this merely additive form either, according to [2]. For a view of the subject involved in an experience doesn't present the subject as something distinct from the experience in such a way that there's any sense in which I can be said to observe the subject, on the one hand, and the experience, on the other hand. Hume expresses this last point by saying that there's a fundamental sense in which what I observe or catch is just the experiencing, the episode of experience

$$\{E\},$$

but this way of putting things has caused great confusion over the centuries, because a point that Hume takes for granted—reasonably enough, because it's a necessary truth—has been suppressed by influential commentators and consequently discounted by many readers. This is the Experience/Experiencer thesis first mentioned in 2.3: the point (the necessary truth) that an experience is an experience, i.e. an experien*cing*. It isn't just an experiential content—not in any sense that allows that an experiential content can somehow concretely exist or occur without an experien*cer*. An experience is a necessarily subject-involving, conscious, contentful mental occurrence. To come across or apprehend an actual experience, an actual episode of experience, an experiencing, is necessarily to come across or apprehend an experiencer, a subject of experience. In Hume's terms: a perception, an actual temporally situated occurrence, a concrete mental event, isn't just a perceptual content. It is, as he says, a *perception*, an actual perceiv*ing* of something by someone or something—a perceiv*er*.

A necessary truth needn't be phenomenologically apparent, even in one who takes it for granted—a point to which I'll return. The present claim is not that Hume takes a certain theoretical point (a necessary truth) for granted and automatically applies it in his report of the deliverances of (present-moment) mental self-examination. Nor is it that Hume's experience of intimate entrance is influenced by his theoretical appreciation of the necessary truth in question. The present claim is just a claim about what he means by the word 'perception' ('experience').

One might express it by saying that {E} can and should be represented as follows:

{S:C},

where 'C' stands as before for occurrent experiential content, and ':' has some kind of intense-intimacy-intimating function that we needn't at present specify further. It's {S:C} that I catch or observe, in some way that doesn't involve any full or explicit differentiation of S and C (see further below), when I catch or observe an experience or experiencing {E} and can observe nothing but {E}. For {E} is {S:C}.[80]

In these terms one might choose to say that the error in the traditional interpretation (especially its 'no ownership' division) is the error of thinking that when Hume says that he 'never can observe anything but the experience', he means that all he encounters when he encounters the experience is

{C},

a 'mere' content (a visual presentation as of a tree in leaf, say) given utterly independently of its being an actual episode of experiencing, utterly independently of its being anyone's experience—even though it is given as a concretely occurring phenomenon. Now it's obviously not possible to log a content only in this way in mental self-examination, but even if it were somehow possible, it wouldn't be to log an experience in the way that concerns Hume in this passage. It wouldn't be to register the phenomenon of an actual perceiving, an actual experiential episode considered specifically as such. It wouldn't be to register it in the way one is bound to register it if one is seriously engaged in the specially focused exercise of mental self-apprehension that Hume is engaged in. The bare content supposedly given for inspection on this account of things would somehow have to be nothing but an abstract object with no position in

---

[80] Recall (p. 63n) that experiential content is wholly internalistically conceived, here, as concrete occurrent mental content. (For those who know about philosophical 'Twins', it's that in respect of which you and your Twin on 'Twin Earth' are, mentally, qualitatively identical.) I'm putting aside questions about the 'attitudinal modality' of the experience (belief, imagining, remembering, etc.). For Hume, I take it, these are part of the experiential content of the experience, i.e. the overall experiential-qualitative character of the experience.

time. This is not what Hume had in mind in talking of coming upon perceptions in mental self-examination. And whatever a bare nothing-but-a-content perception is supposed to be, it can't be a perception in Hume's sense, a real live experiencing, without being subject-involving. Only this can give a content reality in time, make it live (adjective or verb), make it something more than an abstract object.

Those attached to the idea that all Hume claims to come upon, in coming upon {E}, is {C}, may concede the last point—which is a metaphysical point, not a phenomenological one—while continuing to insist that it is just the C-ness of the admittedly necessarily S-involving experience that Hume claims to come upon in claiming to come upon nothing but {E}. They would have it that Hume abstracts away from the necessarily subject-involving reality of the experience considered as a concrete whole, even when engaged in this specially focused act of investigative entry into his own mental being, and somehow considers only the abstract content(-type) C.

The trouble with this is that there is no reason to believe it, and overwhelming reason not to, given Hume's careful investigative project. The view that Hume claims to find bare {C}, rather than live, experi-enced, and thus necessarily subject-involving {C}, seems to be nothing but an old, catchy prejudice; facilitated, perhaps, by the fact, discussed in 2.2 above, that words like 'perception' and many other similar words are naturally taken to have both a concrete-occurrence use and a content-type (abstract-object) use.

The weight of the traditional interpretation is great. In many, 'the contrary notion is . . . riveted in the mind' (167/1.3.14.26). I'll make another attempt to convince doubters at the end of this section. Here it may help to consult the imaginary sub-oyster of Hume's Appendix, a creature that is, he supposes, less sophisticated than an oyster, but is none the less, as he says, a 'thinking being', i.e. an experiencing or conscious being, a subject of experience. It is a thinking being although it has 'only one [experience], as of thirst or hunger'.[81] 'Consider it in that situation', he says. 'Do you conceive any thing but merely that [experience]?' No, he answers. But you do indeed conceive an *experience*, i.e. something that is a conscious episode by definition, an actual episode of experiencing.

---

[81] 634/App§16. Oysters were a popular example, used also by Descartes and Locke.

You do (trivially) conceive or come upon a conscious-thinking-being-involving phenomenon, and hence upon a conscious thinking being (one that you are, in Hume's thought experiment, considering specifically and only in its mental being). And Hume's claim is the same as before: nothing more is given to observation or conception, in the thinking being's being given, than the experiencing. There is nothing that gives reason to believe in any '*self* or *substance*' that endures and could possibly exist apart from the experiencing. But to say this is in no way to say that you do not come upon a thinking being, a thinking being considered in its mental being, when you come upon the experiencing.[82]

If I engage with Hume in the practice of entering intimately into what I call myself, then, I get no view of a bare self—{S}—, a self or subject that isn't having any experience. True. Nor do I get a view of a subject having an experience in which the subject is given apart from the overall experience-event as something clearly distinguishable from it—{S + E}. True. And I certainly don't get any view of some enduring unchanging perfectly simple subject —{S}, as it were, the subject pictured in the Simple Fiction view, the soul beloved of the philosophers he's criticizing—that is fully ontologically distinct from the experience. True. What I come upon is {E}, nothing but {E}, where {E} is {S:C}, a concrete entity, an experiencing-of-a-content-by-an-experiencer. This is certainly not to say that the subject is encountered as some sort of *personalitied entity*, when {E} is come upon. It isn't. Nor is it to say that it's encountered as an explicit object of attention, if this is taken to mean that it has some special, intrinsically separate salience as an object of attention over and above the experience-event considered as a whole. Hume's crucial and wholly correct phenomenological point is, once again, that it isn't encountered in this way. How, then, is it encountered? This question has been well treated in the Phenomenological tradition, as remarked, and I will shortly say more.

Some may think that this account of what Hume is saying is sophistical, or attributes something too complicated to him. In fact, though, all it attributes is phenomenological perspicacity, honesty and accuracy of

---

[82]   The first occurrence of the word 'perception' in the sub-oyster paragraph may seem to invite a type reading—the sub-oyster has only one type of perception—while the second occurrence seems to be part of an invitation to consider one single particular 'token' perception. This isn't any kind of error on Hume's part.

expression; it will look sophistical only to those who have been conditioned by the traditional interpretation of Hume.

—None of this can be right, for Hume says that experiences in a mind may be 'contemporary' as well as successive, and he speaks of experiences 'mingling'. On your view this means that he thinks that there are two (or more) subjects of experience present at that time in a mind—which is absurd.[83]

When Hume uses the words you pick out, he is describing in a certain way the fact that a (single) subject's perceptual experience may be complex, for example when one is having a 'complex impression' of an apple (2/1.1.1.2), or simply experiencing both colour and sound. This must be so, in fact, for if there weren't only one subject there'd be no 'mingling' (1.4.6.4), no experienced contemporariness of the sort that occurs in the complex impression of an apple.[84] These two uses of the word 'perception' are, to that extent, arguably type uses, not token uses, picking out aspects of a single complex perception. But they can equally well be said to be token uses, in as much as a single complex perception can be said to be made up of more than one perception.

Some may now question whether a *subject* is come upon, experientially, when {E} is come upon. What is come upon, they may say, what is knowably come upon, is, at bottom, just *subjectivity*. '{E} is {S:C}' can be allowed to stand as correct, they say, only on condition that one read 'S' simply as 'subjectivity'. Meditators may agree, claiming that an event of experience encountered in attentive meditative mental self-examination presents merely as something that is intrinsically both subjectivity-involving and content-involving, not as something intrinsically subject-involving.[85]

I think this question is worth raising, although there's no reason to think that Hume ever thought along these lines, or ever thought that there could be an experience without a 'thinking being' (there is a thinking being, in his view, even in the case of a sub-oyster). Given the way I understand the

[83] 259/§16, 253/§4. See p. 44 n. 24 above. See also e.g. 237/1.4.5.12, where Hume talks of the taste, smell, colour, and tangibility of a fruit being 'co-temporary in their appearance in the mind'.

[84] Hume isn't considering a case in which we have 'contemporary' perceptions but aren't aware of some of them: 'the perceptions of the mind are perfectly known' (366/2.2.6.2).

[85] See e.g. Shear 1998, Rosch 1997, Stone 1988, 2005. See also Zahavi 2006: 126. Formal meditation isn't at issue here, in fact, because we're concerned with the ordinary person's entering into himself.

term 'subject', however, it reduces to a terminological quibble. For if there is subjectivity then there is also, and trivially, a subject, as I understand the term—though the subject certainly needn't be any sort of enduring or persisting thing. The move from 'subject' to '(mere) subjectivity' involves a weakening only if one supposes that the term 'subject' is more meta-physically committed than the term 'subjectivity'. It may be objected that 'subject' is a count noun, whereas 'subjectivity' is a mass term which is as such intrinsically less metaphysically committed. The objection is reason-able, but I'm happy to define my maximally non-committal use of 'subject' explicitly in terms of 'subjectivity': I'm happy to allow that to say that subjectivity is knowably present or experientially given is already to allow that a subject is knowably present or experientially given, as I understand the term 'subject'. In effect this simply re-expresses the point in 2.3 that experience is necessarily experience-*for*.[86]

More importantly, I take it that this is in line with Hume's way of thinking, for he holds that we have to do with '*a* thinking being', when we contemplate the sub-oyster's experience, even as he rejects the whole traditional metaphysical framework of substance and accident, and to that extent agrees with Kant that in so far as we accept to use the categories of traditional metaphysics at all, we can't even know that the thinking being (which certainly exists) is substantial in nature, and not in some way an accident or property.[87] He doesn't think that any particular traditional substantial metaphysical commitment is built into the admittedly gram-matically substantival noun phrase 'thinking being'. After all, he holds that individual experiential episodes themselves pass the traditional test for being a substance, so far as our knowledge goes.[88] He doesn't worry about the use of the phrase 'thinking being' and he doesn't need to. If

[86] Note that if one allows that there is subjectivity where I am, and non-overlapping subjectivity where you are, and again where your friend is, one is in effect committed to a count noun in any case—something like 'patch of subjectivity', or 'episode' or 'stream' of subjectivity, i.e. *a* subject.

[87] It is, Kant says, 'quite impossible' for me, given my experience of myself as a mental phenomenon, 'to determine the manner in which I exist, whether it be as substance or object or as accident or property' (1787: B420). Compare Hume 233/1.4.5.5. Compare also Descartes's carefully stated position in his *Second Meditation*: 'I know that I exist; the question is, what is this *I* that I know? I do not know. But whatever I suppose, and whatever the truth is, for all that I am still something.' Descartes doesn't at this stage commit himself on the question of ontological category.

[88] 233/1.4.5.5, 635/§19. Hume likes this point.

there is indeed an experience, then there is indeed a thinking being, on his terms—trivially so.[89]

Can't we somehow hold onto the only-{C} reading of 'we never can observe anything but the [experience]'? I think we can, so long as the point that the content is *live* is thought through and fully accepted. It's experienced content, an experiencing; occurrent content, content that is experientially 'had'. When content so understood is encountered, the necessarily existing subject is also encountered {S}, although the subject not figured as {S} in a way that distinguishes it from {E}.

—I'm not so sure. In his discussion of the relation between perceptions and objects in 1.4.2, Hume writes as follows:

as the *appearance* of [an experience] in the mind and its *existence* seem at first sight entirely the same, it may be doubted, whether we can ever assent to so palpable a contradiction, and suppose [an experience] to exist without being present to the mind. In order to clear up this matter, and learn how the interruption in the appearance of [an experience] [to the mind] implies not necessarily an interruption in its existence, 'twill be proper to touch upon some principles, which we shall have occasion to explain more fully afterwards. (206/1.4.2.37)

At this point a footnote refers to 1.4.6, and the passage casts considerable doubt on your claim that Hume never considers the idea that there could be a perception or experience without a perceiver or experiencer; the claim, in other words, that he takes the Experience/Experiencer thesis for granted.

The first thing to say in reply, I think, is that we can draw no clear conclusions about Hume's views on the metaphysics of perceptions from the complications of 1.4.2 (they begin at 193/1.4.2.14). This is especially so given that Hume has at this point, if only temporarily, adopted a way of expounding things which [a] allows and/or obliges him to use 'perception' and 'object' interchangeably, 'understanding by both of them what any common man means by a hat, or shoe, or stone' (202/1.4.2.31), and [b] appears to lead him to suggest that the vulgar, as well as philosophers in ordinary life, think that experiences or perceptions conceived as mental entities are things that continue to exist when unexperienced or unperceived.[90]

[89] For a doubt about this approach to the sub-oyster, see Garrett 1997: 180.

[90] What he has fundamentally in mind is correct; it's the point that we take it that we immediately perceive material objects. The problem is that he has, partly for polemical purposes, chosen to express this in a very confusing way.

Putting that aside, the more substantive point is this. When Hume restates the problem he has raised in the passage just quoted—'How we can satisfy ourselves in supposing a perception to be absent from the mind without being annihilated' (207/1.4.2.38)—he briefly mentions the bundle theory in his answer, anticipating 1.4.6. The reason we can entertain such a supposition, he says, is that 'what we call a *mind*, is nothing but a heap or collection of different perceptions, united together by certain relations' (207/1.4.2.39). But his point is not that there can be a perceiving/perception without a perceiver (a 'palpable contradiction'). His point (which he makes in several other places, e.g. 233/1.4.5.5, 244/1.4.5.24, 252/§3, 635/App§19) is rather that a single perception could for all we know possibly exist all on its own, i.e. not as part of something larger, i.e. what we ordinarily think of as a mind, or as, necessarily, a property of a mind. This point is greatly strengthened if the 'true idea' of a mind has it that a mind is nothing but 'a connected heap of perceptions'. Hence the reference forward to 1.4.6, where he is going to argue just this. But there is no challenge here to the Experience/Experiencer thesis. Every perception must of course involve a perceiver. The claim is just that a perception needn't be a state or property (or part) of a thing lasting longer than it does, i.e. a mind as standardly conceived.

2.15 'When I enter most intimately into what I call *myself*' 2

In 2.8 I introduced the ESC thesis, the metaphysical thesis that an experience necessarily involves a subject of experience as well as a content, and represented it as follows:

$$[E \rightarrow [S \& C]].$$

It's natural to ask how this straightforwardly metaphysical claim relates to the structurally cognate phenomenological claim, made in the last section, that an event of experience genuinely grasped in mental self-examination presents as both subject-involving and content-involving, which I've represented as

$$\{E\} = \{S:C\}.$$

I'll consider this question now, both for its own sake and for the further light it throws on Hume's position.

Let me first strengthen the representation of the metaphysical ESC thesis to bring it formally into line with the phenomenological thesis as follows:

$$[E = S:C].$$

This states that an experience (a Humean perception) consists, metaphysically, of a subject entertaining, experiencing, standing in the relation of haver-of to, . . . , an experiential content.[91] I think that this is in fact the best—right—thing to say, when the notion of the subject is being taken in Hume's way, i.e. narrowly and mentalistically, as it is here; but one needn't accept this in order to consider the question of how the two claims, curly and straight bracketed, phenomenological and metaphysical, relate.[92]

It may first be said that the phenomenological claim can be false even if the metaphysical claim is true. It may be said that even if [E = S:C] is true it's possible to have an experience—of a tree, say—and to be aware of it specifically as an experience, an occurring experiential content (so that one isn't merely engaged with the outside world), without being *in any way* aware of the subject of experience, let alone necessarily aware of it; so that in this case {E} is just {C}.

I think this claim may still sound plausible to some in the analytic tradition, and some non-philosophers may agree. But even if it's true (I'll consider it further below), it isn't relevant to the present discussion of Hume. For the question that concerns us at present isn't just about having an—any—experience which involves some sort of awareness of an experience. It's much more specific. It's about what happens when, like Hume, one goes in pursuit of a certain specially focused kind of experience: when one sets out specifically to observe oneself having an experience and in this way 'enters intimately' and attentively into oneself.

---

[91] The intimacy-intimating colon is designed to sweep up all these phrases; different theories may give different accounts of its force, which is now metaphysical, not phenomenological.

[92] I argue for this in Strawson 2003. With the William James of *The Principles of Psychology*, I think that the best thing to say, when we operate with the 'thin', mentalistic notion of the subject, is that every numerically distinct experience has a different subject. As it stands, however, the symbolism doesn't exclude saying that numerically distinct experiences occurring in a human being have the same subject. Thus we might have $[E_1 = S_1:C_1]$, $[E_2 = S_1:C_2]$, $[E_3 = S_1:C_3]$, and so on.

It's about what one finds, in the way of mental phenomena, when one does this rather unusual thing. And here I think it's clear that to log the experiencing properly—genuinely to grasp something as an experience, i.e. as an experiencing—is, necessarily, to log the experiencer in some way. For the experience consists of an experiencer experiencing an experiential content, and focused attention to it—to the experience considered specifically as an episode of experience—is bound to be cognizant of this fact in some manner or other. This is so even if the focused attention needn't involve any explicit grasp of the fact that the experiencer is oneself. It's so even if (even though) it needn't involve any thought of the sort that is characteristic—definitive—of full or express self-consciousness.[93]

This may still be doubted, so let me restate the point (first in an intentionally imperfect way). The claim is not that the subject (the subject-as-such, as it were) must present (verb) as an explicit object of attention: it's not that the subject must be expressly apprehended in an explicit or (in Phenomenological, and specifically Sartrean terminology) *thetic* or *positional* way as something in the 'focus' of consciousness or attention. On the contrary: it seems clear that the best thing to say in many contexts, given the way in which the conception of what it would be to apprehend the (mental) subject is set up in those contexts, is that the subject isn't apprehended—not even in a specially attentive act of Humean mental self-examination. Even in this case any awareness of the subject is likely to be entirely non-thetic in Sartre's sense, in no way explicitly articulated. Many sincere self-observers will accordingly truthfully deny that they encounter any such thing as the subject in the Humean experiment at all, and they'll be right. This is the sense in which Hume's phenomenological report, according to which all he finds is $\{E\}$, is entirely correct. There is indeed no thetic presentation of the subject as such, even in focused mental self-examination, for any such presentation would have to be presentation of the subject as something distinct from the experience as a whole—this is what a thetic focusing of attention on the subject would inevitably amount to—and this, as Hume rightly says, is precisely what doesn't happen.

---

[93]   By full or express self-consciousness I mean consciousness of oneself thought of specifically *as oneself* (see e.g. Locke *Essay* 2.27.9). For the familiar point that this is a distinct way of thinking of oneself, see e.g. Castañeda 1966, Shoemaker 1968, Perry 1979.

There is, nevertheless, awareness of the subject, or so I propose. Successful, attentive focusing on the whole phenomenon of an experience, an actual episode of experiencing, can't deliver just the content of the experience, any more than successful focusing on the whole phenomenon of a page with words written on it can deliver just the content of the words. And in fact the last paragraph is too concessive. The concession lies in the fact that the notion of being apprehended as an explicit object of attention is being taken to be equivalent to the notion of being apprehended as an explicit *and distinct* object of attention. But we needn't accept this. An aspect of a complex phenomenon can be explicitly apprehended without being taken as a distinct object of attention (we may be said to explicitly apprehend the redness and roundness and other features of the ball without taking any of them singly as distinct objects of attention). There's a fundamental sense in which the subject is indeed an explicit object of my attention, and necessarily so, when I apprehend the experience as a whole taken explicitly as such, i.e. as an experience, in focused present-moment mental self-examination— simply because the experience I apprehend is indeed an experience, i.e. an experienc*ing*, a necessarily subject-involving thing (not just a content). I can't possibly genuinely apprehend it as such, as an experiencing, without *ipso facto* apprehending the subject that is necessarily involved in the experiencing.

It may be said that even if this is so—even if I do necessarily apprehend the subject, in apprehending an experience in focused mental self-examination, and even if there's a sense in which I apprehend the subject explicitly in so doing, although I don't apprehend it as a distinct object of attention— still I don't explicitly apprehend the subject *as such* as part of the object of my attention, in apprehending the experience explicitly as an experience. And it may then be said that this *as-such-ness* is central to one conception of what explicitness is. But this claim, too, is debatable. It brings up the distinctness issue again, because there are two readings of 'apprehend as such'. Thus it may be reasonably said that although I don't apprehend the subject explicitly as such as the object of my attention by any process of consciously deploying a *concept* of the subject, I do none the less apprehend the subject explicitly as such in apprehending what is in fact the object of my attention—the experience, the experiencing—explicitly *as an experience*, an experiencing; and even though I don't apprehend the subject as in any way distinct from the whole experiencing. And I think this is right.

2.16 Awareness of awareness; self-awareness

—I understand your phenomenological claim, and I still don't agree with it. The claim that you can't observe an experience without also observing an experiencer is doubtless true when taken merely referentially or 'relationally': if an experience consists metaphysically of a subject experiencing a content, then of course awareness of an experience is necessarily awareness of a subject. But why should I accept the claim when it's taken 'notionally', i.e. as a phenomenological claim, a claim about the experiential character that my experience has for me when I set out on the Humean project of focused present-moment mental self-examination and deliberately take one of my experiences as the object of my attention?[94]

I do mean it to be taken 'notionally' or phenomenologically, and not just referentially or relationally. Perhaps it will help to distinguish two versions of the phenomenological claim, i.e. the claim that any conscious mental episode whose principal phenomenological content is such that it is

[i] awareness of an experience

will also and necessarily be such that its phenomenological content involves

[ii] awareness of a subject of experience,

even though [ii] need not (and this is Hume's point) involve any presentation of the subject as a distinct object of awareness, and may amount simply to a genuine grasp of the fact that the experiential content is live, is being lived, had, experienced.

The first and weaker version of this claim restricts attention to those cases in which one has, with Hume, undertaken to engage in the special attentive activity of entering intimately into what one calls oneself. The second and stronger version has it that any mental episode at all whose primary content is [i]—and it's plain that such episodes can occur even when one isn't involved in specially focused and intentionally directed intimate self-examination—necessarily involves [ii]; however non-thetic the awareness of the subject may be.

I think we should all grant the first, weaker version of the claim, and I think that it's the beginning of wisdom in these matters to see that the second is also true.[95] The simplest way to realize this, perhaps, is to

---

[94] For the relational–notional distinction see Quine 1955; remember that phenomenological content properly understood is no less cognitive than sensory (p. 38).

[95] Note that it applies at least as well in the case of experiences that are not one's own (although this doesn't concern us here) as in the case of experiences that are one's own.

consider the difference between what it is to think clearly of or otherwise apprehend a patch of red and what it is to think clearly of or otherwise apprehend a (one's) thought or experience of a patch of red.[96]

Many philosophers favour a third and far stronger phenomenological claim, which I mentioned earlier and put aside: the claim that absolutely all experiences necessarily involve some sort of non-thetic but none the less phenomenologically real awareness, on the part of the subject of awareness, of itself as subject; simply in so far as they necessarily involve some sort of awareness of awareness. This claim can seem very implausible, when we consider that very primitive organisms may have experience, although the parallel non-phenomenological or merely relational claim (all awareness of awareness involves awareness of the subject of awareness) seems hard to deny, given the fundamental sense in which one can't be aware of a property of a thing without *ipso facto* being aware of that thing.

Let me expand this very briefly. There is, it seems, an undeniable (if initially difficult) sense in which

[iii] all awareness (consciousness) either involves or is inevitably accompanied by some sort of awareness (consciousness) of that awareness (consciousness).

I'll call this the *Awareness of Awareness* thesis, the *AA* thesis for short. Hume is one of many who subscribes to it, following Aristotle, Arnauld, Descartes, and Locke among others. He claims, for example, that 'all actions and sensations of the mind are known to us by consciousness' (190/1.4.2.7).[97]

---

[96] Harry Frankfurt provided this simple and I think decisive case during a discussion at Princeton in 2001.

[97] On the AA Thesis see further Woodruff-Smith 1989: ch. 2, Gallagher and Zahavi 2008: ch. 3. According to Aristotle, 'if we perceive, we perceive that we perceive, and if we think, that we think' (*c*.350 BCE: *Nicomachean Ethics* 9.9.1170a29-b1). Descartes uses the term 'thought' 'to apply to all that exists within us in such a way that we are immediately conscious of it ... thus all the operations of the will, the intellect, the imagination and the senses are thoughts' (1641–2: 2.116); 'we cannot', he says, 'have any thought of which we are not aware at the very moment when it is in us' (1641–2: 2.171). Arnauld holds that 'thought or perception is essentially reflective on itself, or, as it is said more aptly in Latin, *est sui conscia* [is conscious of itself]. For I am never thinking without knowing that I am thinking' (1683: 71). Locke, also using 'think' and 'perceive' in the general Cartesian way, says that consciousness 'is inseparable from thinking, and, as it seems to me, essential to it: it being impossible for any one to perceive without perceiving that he does perceive' (*Essay* 2.27.9). Note that it would be anachronistic to suppose that when Aristotle, Locke, Arnauld, and

The AA thesis has a weaker version, in which it's asserted only of creatures capable of full or express self-consciousness (p. 86) in the way that we are, as well as the stronger version, i.e. [iii], in which it's asserted of any experiencer at all, and therefore of creatures that we don't suppose to be capable of express self-consciousness, e.g. spiders and sea snails (assuming that there is something it is like to be them, experientially speaking). I think a number of analytic philosophers are still inclined to reject even the weaker version of the AA thesis, let alone the stronger version, which also has powerful defenders. Perhaps the first thing to say is that neither is refuted by the case in which one is absorbed in a thrilling book or film or game.

The AA thesis is a common topic of discussion in philosophy in the eighteenth century, and there are two main schools of thought among those who accept it—'higher-order' theorists and 'same-order' theorists—just as there are today. The overall situation is complex. Here let me say only that while some higher-order theorists think that all awareness is accompanied by a distinct higher-order awareness of that awareness,[98] same-order theorists think that all awareness intrinsically or constitutively involves awareness of that very awareness. On the whole, Leibniz appears to be a clear supporter of the higher-order view; Descartes, Arnauld, and Locke support the same-order view. Locke, for example, claims that 'thinking *consists* in being conscious that one thinks'—just as 'hunger consists in that very sensation' (*Essay* 2.1.19). Descartes specifies that 'the initial thought by means of which we become aware of something does not differ from the second thought by means of which we become aware that we were aware of it, any more than this second thought differs from the third thought by means of which we become aware that we were aware that we were aware' (1641–2: 2.382).

So much, very briefly, for the AA thesis, to which we may now add the thesis that

Descartes say that we perceive *that* we perceive, this shows that they must think that this involves some sort of expressly propositional apprehension (Locke, for one, certainly holds that a creature can perceive without possessing the concept of perceiving).

[98] This characterization excludes present-day higher-order theorists of consciousness like Rosenthal, who hold that conscious awareness is essentially constituted by one mental state's being the object of another, where neither state taken in isolation involves any sort of conscious awareness (see e.g. Rosenthal 1986, 2009).

[iv] all experience or consciousness or awareness of any kind on the part of any sentient creature, involves some sort of awareness, on the part of that creature, of itself.

I'll call this the *All Awareness involves Self-Awareness* thesis, the *ASA* thesis for short. There is as remarked a straightforward non-phenomenological sense in which the ASA thesis follows immediately from the AA thesis, given that all awareness is awareness on the part of a subject, and that there's a fundamental respect in which to be aware of a property of something is necessarily to be aware of that thing. The question is whether the ASA thesis is any kind of phenomenological truth.

Gurwitsch gives a very good statement of the AA thesis in a paper which argues that the ASA thesis doesn't follow from the AA thesis when the ASA thesis is taken to involve thetic or 'positional' or attentive awareness of the subject, awareness of the subject figured specifically as such. Ordinary experience, he points out, is wholly 'non-egological' in Sartre's terms, i.e. not in any way thetic with respect to the subject:

the subject in his dealing with the object, aware as he is of this dealing, is nevertheless in no way aware of his ego, much less of his ego's involvement in his dealing. (1941: 327)

Consciousness... is consciousness of an object on the one hand and an inner awareness of itself on the other hand. Being confronted with an object, I am at once conscious of this object and aware of my being conscious of it. This awareness in no way means reflection: to know that I am dealing with the object which, for instance, I am just perceiving, I need not experience a second act bearing upon the perception and making it its object. In simply dealing with the object I am aware of this very dealing.[99]

True. But it doesn't follow, from the fact that the subject isn't thetically or 'positionally' apprehended in everyday experience, that there's no sense in which it is genuinely phenomenologically apprehended in everyday experience. Still less does it follow that there's no sense in which it's

---

[99] Ibid 330. Aristotle makes a similar point: 'knowledge and perception and opinion and understanding have always something else as their object, and themselves only by the way or *en passant* or *en marge*' (*c.*350 BCE: *Metaphysics* 12.9.1074b35–6). See also Kriegel 2004: 200: 'it is impossible to think or experience something consciously... without being peripherally aware of thinking or experiencing it'. Note that Gurwitsch's 'aware of my being conscious of it' is better put impersonally as 'aware of *there* being consciousness of it'. The 'my' is merely referential or relational, not part of the explicit or notional content of the awareness, and Gurwitsch restates the point impersonally or non-egologically in the last sentence of the quotation, speaking of 'this very dealing'.

apprehended in focused present-moment mental self-examination. We know Hume accepts some version of the AA thesis, holding that 'all actions and sensations of the mind are known to us by consciousness' (190/1.4.2.7), and can therefore have no quarrel with the non-phenomenological or merely relational version of the ASA thesis, which follows immediately from the AA thesis. The question which remains, again, is whether he accepts any *phenomenological* version of the ASA thesis, according to which all awareness involves or is accompanied by some sort of phenomenological self-awareness.

It may be thought that an affirmative answer to the question follows immediately from his claim that 'when my [experiences] are remov'd for any time, as by sound sleep; so long am I *insensible of **myself**' (252/§3). For this passage suggests that Hume thinks that to be having an experience at all is to be in some way phenomenologically sensible of oneself understood as a mental entity, whether or not one is engaged in mental self-examination. To that extent it provides further support for the view that he doesn't think that coming across nothing but an experience when engaged in the special activity of mental self-examination is a matter of

[v] *not* coming across the self or subject = oneself considered as a mental something in any phenomenological sense at all

even though it's certainly not a matter of

[vi] coming across a/the self or subject *phenomenologically presented as something distinct from the experience.*

Strictly speaking, however, the passage says only that I'm not sensible of myself (i.e. myself mentally considered) when sound asleep, not that I'm always and necessarily sensible of myself when awake and having experience, and it can be given a wholly non-phenomenological reading, however implausible such a reading is in the case of Hume's text.

We can bring in other supporting passages, such as those in which he speaks of '...ourself, of whom we are every moment conscious' (340/2.2.2.17), or says that 'ourself is always intimately present to us' (320/2.1.11.8); but really there's no need. It seems useful to lay out the AA thesis and the ASA thesis, but the basic case was made in the last two sections. In so far as the experience/experiencing is genuinely phenomenologically given in focused present-moment mental self-examination, so too the self or subject is genuinely phenomenologically given; although, again, it is not given as something distinct from the experience.

To say this is not to say or imply that Hume thinks that mental self-examination warrants anything more than the bundle theory. The claim is only that he apprehends the things in the bundle as they are, in their experiential reality, not just as bare contents, but as live, necessarily subject-involving entities. He doesn't think that the experience of experience that is yielded by focused present-moment mental self-examination is experience of mere bare content, rather than experience of live content, subject-of-experience-involving content, hence experience of a, or the, subject of experience in action. He doesn't think that you don't come across a subject in coming across an experience/experiencing, although he's quite sure that you don't come across anything that gives you any reason to believe in the unchanging persisting subject of the philosophers and the church.

If I can't convince you, perhaps Russell can. He considers the Humean project of mental self-examination and makes the point most helpfully in his own terms in *The Problems of Philosophy*:

When we try to look into ourselves we always seem to come upon some particular thought or feeling, and not upon the 'I' which has the thought or feeling. Nevertheless there are some reasons for thinking that we are acquainted with the 'I', though the acquaintance is hard to disentangle from other things. To make clear what sort of reason there is, let us consider for a moment what our acquaintance with particular thoughts really involves. When I am acquainted with 'my seeing the sun', it seems plain that I am acquainted with two different things in relation to each other. On the one hand there is the sense-datum which represents the sun to me, on the other hand there is that which sees [has] this sense-datum. All acquaintance ... seems obviously a relation between the person acquainted and the object with which the person is acquainted. When a case of acquaintance is [itself something] with which I can be acquainted (as I am acquainted with my acquaintance with the sense-datum representing the sun) it is plain that the person acquainted is myself. Thus, when I am acquainted with my seeing the sun, the whole fact with which I am acquainted is 'Self-acquainted-with-sense-datum'.... It does not seem necessary to suppose that we are acquainted with a more or less permanent person, the same today as yesterday, but it does seem as though we must be acquainted with that thing, whatever its nature, which sees the sun and has acquaintance with sense-data. Thus, in some sense it would seem we must be acquainted with our Selves as opposed to our particular experiences.[100]

---

[100] 1912: 27–8; Sydney Shoemaker tells me that this passage was the subject of his first paper, and it's worth bearing in mind Shoemaker's demolition of the 'view, which motivates "bundle", "logical construction", and "no subject" theories of the self, that from an empiricist standpoint the status of the self (the subject of experience) is suspect compared with that of

And when John Foster writes that

> a natural response to Hume would be to say that, even if we cannot detect ourselves *apart from* our perceptions (our conscious experiences), we can at least detect ourselves *in* them—that when I introspectively detect an experience, what is revealed is the complex of myself-experiencing-something or myself-experiencing-in-a-certain-manner. Indeed, it is not clear in what sense an experience *could* be introspectively detected without the detection of its subject (1991: 215; see also 215–19)

his only error, perhaps, is to suppose that Hume thought otherwise. Hume's target was the simple unchanging persisting subject beloved of his contemporaries, nothing less and nothing more.[101]

2.17 Is Hume right about intimate entrance?

How does Hume come out of all this? Wonderfully well. He makes an extremely perceptive claim—a completely accurate claim, as far as I can see—about what it's actually like to encounter oneself as a (mental) subject of experience when one has decided to go looking for oneself considered specifically as a (mental) subject of experience.

How does one do this? The most natural thing to do is to try to catch oneself on the fly in one's experience in the present moment. (It's a familiar point that the act of trying to make one's present experience the explicit or thetic object of one's attention induces a delay which means that what one actually catches is the immediate past experience.)[102] And this, I take it, is what Hume did. There is, as he says, [1] no bare or naked view or apprehension of the subject. There is, as he says, [2] no view or

such things as sensations, feelings, images, and the like' (1986: 24). At the same time, Shoemaker thinks that the standard perceptual model of introspection favoured by such empiricists is incorrect, and his claim is accordingly conditional: *if* one accepts such a model at all then 'the view that we have introspective perception of individual mental happenings but not of a self is indefensible' (ibid.).

[101]   Objection: 'I still favour the only-{C} reading because I think that Hume might have been happy to agree with what Kant is trying to express when he says such things as that "the representation of [empirical] apperception is nothing more than feeling of an existence" (1783: §46n), or that "the consciousness of myself in the representation *I* is no intuition at all, but a merely *intellectual* representation of the self-activity [*Selbsttätigkeit*] of a thinking subject"' (Kant 1781/7: B228). Reply: to the extent that this is right, it seems to me to strengthen the rejection of the only-{C} reading.

[102]   At least in normal circumstances; see Strawson 2010.

apprehension of the subject as co-occurrent with the episode of experiencing considered as a whole but in some way saliently experientially distinct from it. There is, as he says, [3] nothing that presents both as the subject of the apprehended experience and as an intrinsically persisting (or in any way experience-transcendent) thing. There is, nevertheless (and of course), [4] apprehension of the subject of experience, not only 'relationally' speaking but also 'notionally' speaking (p. 88), in the apprehension of the experience in present-moment mental self-examination. One may also conduct one's investigation by having, or staging, in expressly introspective mode, an individual, explicitly self-conscious mental episode; by thinking, now, 'I'm reading a book' or 'I'm bored', 'I'm now thinking about my thinking'. I have no reason to think that Hume did this, but the result is the same, although the occurrence of a reference to 'I' in the explicit content of the thought may at first make it seem otherwise.

To say that the self or mental subject doesn't present as an intrinsically persisting thing is not to say that people don't believe that it's an intrinsically persisting thing. They do, as Hume knows. They may well also believe that they have direct experience of there being such a thing, or at least experience that strongly backs up the belief that there is such a thing—as Hume also remarks.[103] If, however, we consider how the mental subject is given in studied but unprejudiced mental reflection of the sort Hume is engaged in, we find nothing of the sort, as he says. This, after all, is why he devotes most of 'Of personal identity' to explaining the mechanisms by which we come to believe in a persisting subject of experience in spite of the fact that no such thing presents itself as such when we engage in reflection of this kind.[104]

2.18 Hume and James

The Appendix beckons. I'll approach it via William James, replacing his Cartesian, catch-all use of the words 'thought' and 'thinker' with my catch-all words 'experience' and 'experiencer' or 'subject of experience'.[105]

---

[103] Three years earlier, Butler calls our knowledge of our personal identity (over time) 'that certain conviction, which necessarily and every moment rises within us, when we turn our thoughts upon ourselves, when we reflect upon what is past, and look forward upon what is to come' (1736: 447; see also p. 53 n. 37 above, and Thiel 2011: ch. 8).

[104] The natural 'fiction' of a persisting self is of course something very much less than the idea of an immortal immaterial soul.

[105] James explicitly follows Descartes in using 'thought' as a general word for conscious mental episodes. See James 1890: 1.186, 1.224.

According to James, the self or subject or '*I*'

... is an [experience], at each moment different from that of the last moment, but appropriative of the latter, together with all that the latter called its own. All the experiential facts [of mental life] find their place in this description, unencumbered with any hypothesis save that of the existence of passing [experiences].[106]

His claim in *The Principles of Psychology* is not just that this is all we have empirical evidence for, so far as the existence of subjects or selves is concerned. As it stands, his claim is that this is all there is. He isn't of course proposing that there are only experiences and no experiencers. His view is precisely that 'the [experiences] themselves are the [experiencers]'.[107]

This isn't the incoherent claim that the experiencer is itself nothing but an experiential content whose existence involves no experiencing. The word 'experience' ('thought') denotes a necessarily subject-involving episode of experiencing, not just an experiential content conceived of as somehow (impossibly) occurring without any experiencer of it.

James's proposal may seem very odd; it takes time to come to appreciate it—to grasp its cogency. In effect it's the same as the proposal that [E = S:C]— which may have sounded at least a little less odd, when it came up on page 85, than the claim that the experiences themselves are the experiencers.

The role James gives to the brain should further diminish the sense of oddness. For although he proposes that there are many numerically distinct successive selves, in the case of a human being, he takes it that there's only one brain. 'The same brain', he says, 'may subserve many conscious selves' that 'have no substantial identity':[108]

successive [experiencers], *numerically distinct*, but all aware of the past in the same way, form an adequate vehicle for all the experience of personal unity and sameness which we actually have.[109]

Such successive experiencers—successive patches of neural activity that are conscious events—are not only all that we have empirically respectable evidence for, when we look for something that might qualify as the

---

[106] 1892: 191, 1890: 1.400–01. He makes the same point in other terms in 1890: 1.338–42.

[107] 'The thoughts themselves are the thinkers' (1892: 191).

[108] 1890: 1.401; 1892: 181.

[109] 1892: 181. Compare Damasio 1994: 236–43: 'at each moment the state of self is constructed, from the ground up. It is an evanescent reference state, so continuously and consistently reconstructed that the owner never knows that it is being remade unless something goes wrong with the remaking' (p. 240).

persisting inner mental subject; they're also all we need to posit in order to account for all the mental appearances, on James's view, including (nb) the appearances that, in his opinion, make his famous metaphor of the stream of consciousness apt as a description of the character of our experience. In particular, we don't need to postulate a continuing self or subject to account for the evident connections between the experiences of an individual human being; and in fact short-lived successive selves are all there are, in James's proposal: the short-lived subjects of experience intrinsic to the successive experiences that arise constantly in the brain.

James, then, puts forward a version of the 'Transience' view, according to which an inner mental 'I' or subject or self is

[−A]   something that has *short-term* existence
[+B]   a diachronically *non-compound* thing, 'a single pulse of subjectivity' (1890: 1.278)
[+C]   a diachronically *continuous* thing.[110]

He's motivated by a radical form of empiricism that I believe to be indefensible, but that is no grounds for an objection to the substance of his proposal.

2.19 The brain

—Doesn't the principle of abduction, the principle of inference to the best explanation, very strongly favour the hypothesis of some sort of continuing self or subject, when applied to the phenomenon of the evident connection between the experiences of an individual human being?

James sees no reason to think so, and he's right, on his terms, because he has a further fundamental resource, over and above the successive experiences of an individual human being, when it comes to explaining the connection between those experiences. He has the brain, in which we may say that all the experiences occur or 'reside'. This is a resource which Hume crucially lacks, or rather puts aside (for he is in fact a materialist), in his discussion of the self in the *Treatise*. It may be added that Hume's empiricist principles debar him from any use of arguments to the best explanation, which necessarily (by definition) go beyond the empirically

---

[110] Note that the Transience view of the self is opposed to the bundle view ([+A −B −C]) on all three counts.

available evidence in their conclusions.¹¹¹ I'll end Part 2 by explaining this a little further.

There are two principal claims before us. The first is that there's no direct empirical *evidence* for a continuing self (or mind). The second is that there's no *need* to posit such a self (or mind) to account for the phenomena. James and Hume are on equal terms when it comes to the point about evidence, but it looks as if Hume is worse off when it comes to the point about need. This, in effect, is what underlies the vanishing of his hopes in the Appendix. For 'it is evident that there is a principle of connexion between the different thoughts or ideas of the mind' (23/3.1), and Hume sees that he needs a continuing entity or something to equivalent effect (e.g. observable 'real connexion'—636/App§21), in order to accommodate this evident fact of connection. The trouble is that no suitable continuing entity (or observable real connection) can have a legitimate place in his philosophy.

James, by contrast, is all right; he has the brain to explain the connection.¹¹² This is why he can dismiss the objection that inference to the best explanation supports the idea of some sort of continuing self or subject, when it comes to explaining the evident connection between the experiences of an individual human being. He doesn't need a continuing self or subject in addition to a continuing brain—any more than one needs a continuing self or subject to explain the massive regularities and connections between a computer's operations from day to day. It's enough for him that short-lived selves, numerically distinct, arise successively from the same brain (from brain conditions that have considerable similarity from moment to moment, even as they change).

It may seem that Hume can also call on the brain. In fact he doesn't need to do so in any way in which he hasn't already done so, by that point in the *Treatise*. In 1.2, when he's discussing the principles of association of ideas, he remarks that he hasn't yet appealed to the functioning of the brain to

---

¹¹¹ This is why he's obliged to classify the product of his transempirical appeal to 'sound reason' as 'incomprehensible', although it is both 'natural' and a matter of sound reason (48/1.2.4.2; see p. 52 above). So too his never questioned assumption that there is something about the nature of reality given which it is regular in the way that it is, 'those powers and forces, on which this regular course and succession of objects totally depends' (55/5.22): we have no empirically contentful conception of any sort of the nature of power, which is therefore 'incomprehensible'.

¹¹² He's all right in 1890. His later, 'radical' empiricism may cause problems for him.

explain the operation of the principles. He might very well have done so, he says; but he has so far (and as a good Newtonian) restricted his attention strictly to the observable phenomena of association. Now, though, he says, he 'must here have recourse' to the brain, 'in order to account for the mistakes' that occur in the operation of the principles of association of ideas. Why do mistakes occur?

the mind is endow'd with a power of exciting any idea it pleases; whenever it dispatches the . . . animal . . . spirits into that region of the brain, in which the idea is plac'd; these spirits always excite the idea, when they run precisely into the proper trace, and rummage that cell, which belongs to the idea. But as their motion is seldom direct, and naturally turns a little to one side or the other; for this reason the animal spirits, falling into the contiguous traces, present other related ideas in lieu of that which the mind desir'd at first to survey. (60/1.2.5.20)

Here Hume makes explicit use of the hypothesis that the mind is based in the brain, and claims that he must do so. He can't, however, call on this in the much more radical dialectical context of 1.4.6, 'Of personal identity'. The brain is a physical object, and Hume can't appeal to it after the notion that physical objects might be different from perceptions has been classified as unintelligible in 1.4.2 (and after the causal power whose existence manifests itself in constant conjunction has suffered the same treatment in 1.3.14). He has on his own terms to abide by the same rules of engagement in his treatment of the mind.

PART 3

Hume's Appendix

It is evident that there is a principle of connexion between the
different thoughts or ideas of the mind.

Hume 1748: 23/3.1

3.1 What is Hume's problem?

When Hume returns to the topic of personal identity in the Appendix to
his *Treatise* he summarizes the argument of section 1.4.6, 'Of personal
identity', and restates its conclusion as follows:

the thought alone finds personal identity, when reflecting on the train of past
perceptions, that compose a mind, the ideas of them are felt to be connected
together, and naturally introduce each other.[1]

This is already a little hard to understand, even with an added comma—

the thought alone finds personal identity, when, reflecting on the train of past
perceptions that compose a mind, the ideas of them are felt to be connected
together, and naturally introduce each other

—but what it says, I believe, is this. In so far as we encounter a putative
single persisting self or mind at all, in our experience of ourselves (in so far
as we encounter 'personal identity' at all in our experience of ourselves),
we do so only in so far as we *feel* our past experiences to be connected
together, and in consequence take them to be features or parts of a single

---

[1] 635/App§20. In Part 3 I revert to using Hume's own word 'perception' when quoting
him, while continuing to use 'experience' myself.

persisting entity.[2] There's no impression or direct experience of a persisting self. It's only 'thought' that 'finds' a persisting self; a persisting self is encountered in experience only in the sense that it's a hypothesis or 'fiction' we naturally come up with and believe in and that goes beyond what is empirically given and warranted. The posit-happy, 'fiction'-generating Imagination (see p. 56), receiving as input data nothing more than a series of distinct and separate experiences, reacts in such a way that one comes to believe one has direct experience of a single persisting self or mind. One's Imagination operates in this case in very much the same way as it operates when one reacts to a stream of distinct and separate experiences by coming to believe one has direct experience of enduring physical objects. In both cases it goes beyond the data.

It may be that one's experiences are in fact all 'located' in, or aspects or attributes of, some unknown single persisting thing; Hume records this metaphysical possibility in the Appendix (636/§21). We can't, however, know that this is how things are. Nor can we have any clear or distinct idea of what this single persisting thing might concretely amount to, any more than we can have a clear or distinct idea of what an external physical object is, when we naturally (and indeed inevitably) think of the world as containing such objects; for 'the essence of the mind [is] unknown': it's 'equally unknown to us with that of external bodies' (xvii/Int§8). We are in any case debarred from allowing any such idea of a single persisting thing to feature in a philosophically legitimate definition of what the mind is. 'Our idea of any mind is only that of particular perceptions', according to Hume's empiricism (658/Abs§28).

The same goes for the other metaphysical possibility that Hume considers in the Appendix: the possibility that these successive experiences are indeed ontically distinct things, but are none the less linked by some 'real connexion' (636/App§21), some 'real bond' (259/§15), some connection or bond that is objectively real, not just a subjective feeling on our part, or a posit generated by the Imagination. No idea of a connection or union or bond that is real in this sense can feature in any empiricistically acceptable

---

[2] See p. 36 above for the point that the pronoun 'our' in 'our past experiences' doesn't presuppose what is being denied. I will use the pronoun 'one' in a corresponding way.

statement or definition of what the mind is, because it's not something that is or can be given in experience.[3]

It's not as if we don't really have distinct ideas of the things mentioned in the last two paragraphs:

we have a distinct idea of an object, that remains invariable and uninterrupted thro' a suppos'd variation of time.[4]

We also have

a distinct idea of several different objects existing in succession, and connected together by a close relation.[5]

There's no problem with these ideas as such. They're 'perfectly distinct' (253/§6). It's just that, given the data of experience, they can have no 'intelligible' or understandable *application to concrete reality*, i.e. no genuinely/empirically concretely conceivable application to concrete reality—either in the particular case of the mind or in general. The enduring single mind or self, in so far as it's something we can be said to encounter in experience at all, is just an Imagination-generated construct or posit or 'fiction'. It has no empirically respectable warrant; it's not given in the actual data of experience considered independently of the transformative workings of the Imagination.

Up to this point in the Appendix, all is well and good. Hume has simply summarized his original account of personal identity in 1.4.6 of Book 1 of the *Treatise*. But in the next paragraph he says that it's 'very defective'.

In order to explain why it's defective he first summarizes it again, in four sentences:

If perceptions are distinct existences, they form a whole only by being connected together. But no connexions among distinct existences are ever discoverable by human understanding. We only feel a connexion or a determination of the thought, to pass from one object to another. It follows, therefore, that the thought alone finds personal identity, when reflecting on the train of past perceptions, that

---

[3] Hume's principal example of a 'real connexion' is causal necessity realistically and naively figured as something that exists entirely independently of any construction of the Imagination. See p. 27 n. 43. In the *Enquiries* Hume drops the term 'real connexion' and simply uses 'connexion'.

[4] 253/§6. Note that this is so even if this idea strictly speaking requires a 'fiction'; see 200–01/1.4.2.29.

[5] 253/§6. Nothing essential hangs on the use of the second quotation (should it be thought dubious to link 'real connexion' and 'connected . . . by a close relation').

compose a mind, the ideas of them are felt to be connected together, and naturally introduce each other. (635/App§20)

He remarks, of this new summary of his theory, that it 'has so far a promising aspect', and then immediately and famously adds:

But all my hopes vanish, when I come to explain the principles, that unite our successive perceptions in our thought or consciousness. I cannot discover any theory, which gives me satisfaction on this head.

In short there are two principles, which I cannot render consistent; nor is it in my power to renounce either of them, viz. *that all our distinct perceptions are distinct existences*, and *that the mind never perceives any real connexion among distinct existences*. Did our perceptions either inhere in something simple and individual, or did the mind perceive some real connexion among them, there wou'd be no difficulty in the case. (635–6/App§20–1)

His hopes vanish. His hopes vanish although he can find nothing wrong with either of his two main claims in 1.4.6, i.e. [a] his account of the content of the empirically warranted idea of the mind or self or person, and [b] his causal psychological account of how it is that we come to believe in a single diachronically persisting mind or self or person in spite of the fact that no such idea of the mind is empirically warranted. So why do his hopes vanish? This question has been the subject of a vast debate.

The short answer is given by changing the 'although' six lines above to 'because'. His problem is precisely the fact that he can't fault either [a] or [b]. But more needs to be said. And the first thing to do, perhaps, is to pick out the two fundamental theoretical principles that Hume says he can't renounce. I'll number them '[P1]' and '[P2]':

[P1] 'all our distinct perceptions are distinct existences' (so far as we know)

and

[P2] 'the mind never perceives any real connexion among distinct existences'.

These principles are very clear, and familiar to any reader of Hume. And there's another thing that's very clear. In the last sentence of the passage just quoted, Hume describes two options that would in his opinion *entirely solve his problem*. The first option is that

[O1] 'our perceptions . . . inhere in something simple and individual'.

The second, to spell it out a little, is that

[O2] our perceptions are distinct existences, and 'the mind perceive[s] some real connexion among them'.

Why would either of these two options solve his problem? Because both can sufficiently ground a fundamental theoretical commitment of his philosophy—his commitment to the real existence and operation of something he's just mentioned,

[P3] 'the principle of connexion, which binds...our particular perceptions... together' (635/App§20)

or (in its plural version)

[P4] 'the principles, that unite our successive perceptions in our thought or consciousness' (636/App§20).[6]

This is the principle (these are the principles) of which he remarks in the first *Enquiry*, in his most direct reference to the question of personal identity, that 'it is evident that there is a principle of connexion between the different thoughts or ideas of the mind'.[7] The trouble is that both options are ruled out for him. They have no empirical warrant. They're philosophically inadmissible from Hume's empiricist point of view. The ideas of real or objective unity or connection that the options appeal to are conceptually clear, as remarked. They're 'perfectly distinct' (253/§6) as far as they go. But they're empirically 'unintelligible' in their application to concrete reality. So Hume can't appeal to them in his account of the nature of the mind. His hopes vanish.

This may not be the best way to put the point. It may be better to say that what happens in the Appendix is that Hume realizes that he has no

---

[6] Both these expressions refer at bottom to the same *explanandum*. The fact that one is singular and the other plural is a potential source of confusion, but the same move between singular and plural occurs early in the *Treatise*, in the passage which introduces the *explanandum*: 'nothing wou'd be more unaccountable than the operations of [the imagination], were it not guided by some *universal principles*, which render it, in some measure, uniform with itself in all times and places. Were ideas entirely loose and unconnected, chance alone wou'd join them; and 'tis impossible the same simple ideas should fall regularly into complex ones (as they commonly do) without some bond of union among them, some associating quality, by which one idea naturally introduces another. *This uniting principle* among ideas...' (10/1.1.4.10).

[7] 23/3.1; see also 50/5.14: 'nature has established *connexions* among particular ideas.... These principles of connexion or association we have reduced to three, namely, **Resemblance**, **Contiguity** and **Causation**; which are the only *bonds* that unite our thoughts together...'.

answer, given his overall theory, to an objection that begins by citing the two options he mentions and then challenges him to deny that at least one of them (or rather, perhaps, the disjunction of them) is in effect built into what he means by 'mind', and is therefore built into what he is really taking to be the 'true idea' of the mind, although they're both excluded from his official account of the 'true idea' of the mind. On this account, Hume realizes that he faces what one might call the *Unanswerable Objection*, which goes something like this:

—Your philosophy taken as a whole commits you, Hume, to a view forbidden by your philosophy. More precisely, it commits you to a choice between one of two views. The first is that the self or mind is something like an ontologically (substantially) simple and individual persisting something, in which successive experiences inhere in such a way that it's not problematic that they're connected or united in the way you take them to be. If you reject this—as you must on your empiricist principles, given which we have (among other things) no warrant for believing in or appealing to the existence of anything that lasts longer than the duration of a single fleeting experience—and hold instead that the mind is something ontologically (substantially) multiple, you're no better off. For then you must hold that the mind is something whose existence involves 'real connexion' (and this is something that you have in effect already done); and also, given your own fundamental empiricist principles, that this real connection is *empirically knowable*, experienceable or perceivable by us. You must hold this because the idea of real connection is in fact built into the conception of mind you make use of in your philosophy, and must be empirically justified in order to be licensed for use. But you must also reject the view that it's empirically knowable, given those same fundamental empiricist principles, and you have indeed done so.

I'll return to this way of putting things. The previous version of the point will do for now, because what I want to stress is this. When Hume tells us what would solve his problem he describes two metaphysical options, one straightforwardly ontological, the other ontological/epistemological, and says that either would do the trick. This is the fact from which any sound interpretation of Hume's Appendix must start.

It may be protested that Hume can't really be saying this, because he takes the idea of a persisting, simple, and individual something and the idea of real connection to be 'unintelligible' *tout court*. But he is saying this. Even those who want to reject the above quotations from 253/§6 in support of the claim that Hume thinks that both these two ideas are 'perfectly distinct' must concede that he is taking these two ideas to be *sufficiently intelligible to be available for use in an informative description of a situation in which he wouldn't face the philosophical difficulty he feels he does face.*[8] For Hume (once again) 'unintelligible' means 'not understandable', 'incomprehensible'. It doesn't mean 'incoherent', and so necessarily non-existent, as it standardly does today in philosophy. It means 'not such that it has any empirically warrantable applicability to concrete reality', hence 'not clear in such a way that it can be appealed to in empiricist philosophy'.

Some students of Hume have difficulty with the idea that he makes any use at all of the idea of objective or real connection. This is understandable, at least at first, but the facts are clear. Consider the following passage from section 1.1.4 of the *Treatise* (already quoted in n. 6 above), in which Hume introduces what is arguably the central theoretical idea in his philosophy, the idea of the connection or association of ideas. If our ideas were 'entirely loose and unconnected', he remarks,

chance alone wou'd join them; and *'tis impossible* the same simple ideas should fall regularly into complex ones (as they commonly do) without some *bond of union* among them, some associating quality, by which one idea naturally introduces another.[9]

In fact, 'the same simple ideas [do] fall regularly into complex ones', and one idea 'naturally introduce[s]' another (11/1.1.4.2). This is what actually happens, and it can't possibly happen, Hume says, unless there exists, as a matter of objective fact, a 'bond of union'—a 'uniting principle', 'principles of union or cohesion'—among our ideas (10/1.1.4.1, 13/1.1.4.6). The 'causes' of this phenomenon—he calls it 'a kind of ATTRACTION', and compares it to gravitational attraction—are he says 'mostly unknown, and must be resolv'd into *original qualities of human nature, which I pretend not to explain*'.[10] But this is not to say that these principles of cohesion aren't real. On the contrary, they are indeed real. They're real in the crucial sense that they aren't merely feelings or posits or fictions generated by the Imagination. It's just that we can't know their nature. All we can know of them are the observable regularities to which they give rise.

Don Garrett states this general point robustly:

---

[8] Compare the move he makes in 1.4.5, discussed on p. 50 above.

[9] 10/1.1.4.1. I consider Hume's observation that these mental connections involve only a 'gentle force', and are not exceptionless, on pp. 140–1 below.

[10] 13/1.1.4.6. He follows Newton, who states the law of gravitational attraction while adding that 'the cause of Gravity . . . I do not pretend to know' (1687: 3.240).

Hume is not forbidden by his empiricist principles from postulating the existence of unperceived *deterministic mechanisms* that would *underlie* the propensities of perceptions to appear in particular ways. He is forbidden by his principles only from trying to specify the nature of those mechanisms [in a way that goes] beyond what experience can warrant. (1997: 171, my emphasis)

I'll return to this quotation, because Garrett believes that it provides grounds for rejecting the present account of Hume's problem in the Appendix.

3.2 Real continuity

Hume, then, thinks that there are two options, two concrete states of affairs, that would solve the problem he faces in the Appendix. The first, to repeat it, is that

[O1] 'our perceptions . . . inhere in something simple and individual' (636/App§21).

This state of affairs would clearly provide a very good general basis or starting point for an account of how our experiences can be connected or united in the way that they 'evidently' are, i.e. connected and united quite independently of any feeling or belief on our part that they are; whatever the further details of the account.

The second is that

[O2] our perceptions are distinct existences, and 'the mind perceive[s] some real connection among them' (636/App§21)

or, rearranged, that

[O2] our perceptions are distinct existences, and there is some real connection among them, which the mind perceives.

This too can provide an excellent grounding for the fact that our experiences are connected or united in the way that they evidently are (i.e. quite independently of any feeling or belief on our part that they are united). For there is in this case a perceived—known—real connection among our experiences, i.e. a connection that isn't just a 'fiction' generated by the operation of the Imagination. In the situation imagined by Hume we'd either actually directly perceive the real connections that concerned us, or we'd perceive real connections that underlay the connections that concerned us. Either way, once we'd perceived real connection, the idea of real connection could be an empirically respectable part of our idea of the mind, and Hume's philosophy would be saved.

What are we to make of this? It seems clear enough. Hume's view is that he has in his philosophy appealed to something more than he can legitimately appeal to, something that he could have without difficulty if he could have either [O1] or [O2], but which he can't have because he can't have either of them. What is this something? It's [P3/P4]. It's the fact that there is a real, 'evident . . . connexion between the different thoughts or ideas of the mind' (23/3.1), a connection which is not a fiction of the Imagination but is rather the *modus operandi* of the Imagination. It's the fact that there are [P4] 'principles, that unite our successive perceptions in our thought', the fact that there is [P3] a 'principle of connexion, which binds . . . particular perceptions . . . together'. These principles are (this principle is) in fact, and as remarked, the central engine of Hume's experimental philosophy. And what he now sees, or believes he sees, is that there is at least one further explanatory or explicative step that he needs to take, or has in effect covertly (and on his own terms illegitimately) taken, if he is to make free use of this theoretical engine in the way he does. And, crucially, it's a further step he believes he must take, or rather has taken, *before* or *by the time that* he reaches the point at which he can simply appeal to the '*original* qualities of human nature, which I pretend not to explain' (13/1.1.4.6).[11]

One could put the point by saying that Hume sees that he is committed to acknowledging the applicability of some sort of positive metaphysical characterization of the *real unity/continuity* of a mind, however general in character it is, in order to ground the use he makes of [P3/P4]. What [O1] and [O2] do, in effect, is offer the two most general metaphysical characterizations there are of the real unity/continuity of a mind.

Another way to put it is this: Hume sees that he can no longer maintain that the idea he calls the 'true idea of the human mind' (261/§19) is the idea of the mind he's actually working with in his philosophy. The idea of the mind he's actually working with seems to contain as an essential part a conception of the mind as involving real continuity, a conception which is banned, ruled out by his official theory-of-ideas-based empiricist principles. The problem doesn't arise for his account of the empirically legitimate

---

[11] The 'before' or 'by the time that' is crucial, given Garrett's objection to the present line of argument, which I'll consider on p. 136 and in 3.14 below.

content of our idea of physical objects or causation, but only for his account of the empirically legitimate content of our idea of the mind.

It is in fact an old idea that Hume relies on a non-regularity-theory notion of causation in his descriptions of the mind. One illustration of the point can be found in the paragraph in which Hume restates his two famous definitions of cause in the *Treatise*. Having given the first definition, he goes on to the second:

If we define a cause to be, *An object precedent and contiguous to another, and so united with it in the imagination, that the idea of the one determines the mind to form the idea of the other, and the impression of the one to form a more lively idea of the other*; we shall make still less difficulty of assenting to this opinion. (172/1.3.14.35)

He continues as follows:

Such an influence on the mind is in itself perfectly extraordinary and incomprehensible; nor can we be certain of its reality, but from experience and observation.

Here Hume says that this 'influence on the mind', which is of course a causal influence, is 'perfectly . . . incomprehensible'—perfectly unintelligible. This is exactly what he always says about causal power, causation conceived of in some essentially non-regularity-theory way. He goes on to say that we can none the less be 'certain of its reality'. *We can be certain of its reality in spite of the fact that it is incomprehensible.* It's true that it is only 'from experience and observation' that we can be certain of its reality, experience and observation that leave it 'incomprehensible'. But we can none the less be certain of its reality. Compare his earlier remark that 'the uniting principle among our internal perceptions is as unintelligible as that among external objects, and is not known to us any other way than by experience' (169/1.3.14.29). The uniting principle is unintelligible, and remains completely unintelligible to us, given that we can know it only by experience. But it is none the less known to us in this way. It is known to exist.[12]

---

[12] Objection: all Hume is saying is that the *constant conjunction* referred to in the second definition is extraordinary and incomprehensible: the constant conjunction between (i) the mind's having experience of constant conjunction (between As and Bs, say) and (ii) the mind's coming to be determined in a certain way (i.e. to form the idea of a B on experiencing an A and the idea of an A on experiencing a B). We have, Hume says, no idea why (i) and (ii) should be constantly conjoined. But this doesn't pose any problem for the view that when it comes to causal connections conceived of in some strong non-regularity-theory way, Hume 'denies even the coherence of any would-be thought about such connexions', in such a way that '*the question of their real existence…cannot even arise*' (Millican 2009: 648, my emphasis).

In coming up with [O1] and [O2] Hume comes up with maximally non-committal specifications of the nature or ground of this real continuity (see 3.14 below). I think that we can for the purposes of discussion take them to be not only mutually exclusive, but also exhaustive of the relevant field of metaphysical possibilities, as Hume does in effect.[13] The problem is that although the specifications are maximally metaphysically non-committal, they're still beyond the bounds of his official empiricist philosophy. For according to that philosophy we can never have empirically respectable grounds for believing in any real continuity that lasts longer than the duration of a single fleeting experience or perception.

The term 'real continuity' is useful, and we can take it to include 'real unity', since continuity is identity, i.e. diachronic identity. It marks the base problem, and I'll return to it. For the moment, I simply want to stress again

---

Hume's position on this particular feature of the mind is the same as his position when he says that reason is 'a wonderful and unintelligible instinct in our souls' (179/1.3.16.9), or that the imagination is 'a kind of magical faculty in the soul which…is…inexplicable by the utmost efforts of human1.1.7.15)./1.1.7.15).

Reply. According to Millican, Hume holds that 'our thoughts are confined within the scope of our ideas' in such a way that 'any coherent thought must ultimately be constituted entirely by impression-copy content': if a thought about something isn't coherent by this standard, as in the case of thought about causal connection conceived of in some non-regularity-theory way, then it isn't really a thought at all; it's a 'would-be thought' about something 'the question of [whose] real existence…cannot even arise' (2009: 647–8). One problem with this is that it seems to rule out Hume's just quoted claims about reason and the imagination. Not only do they fail to express thoughts at all; they're about ('about') things the question of whose real existence cannot even arise. Turning to the immediate issue, Hume's claim that his second definition of cause adduces an 'incomprehensible…influence', we encounter a more specific difficulty. If this particular constant conjunction is held to be incomprehensible, all other constant conjunctions must be held to be equally incomprehensible. For what could ever make one less incomprehensible than another? As Hume says, 'all objects, which are not contrary, are susceptible of a constant conjunction, and as no real objects are contrary…to consider the matter *a priori*, any thing may produce any thing, and… we shall never discover a reason, why any object may or may not be the cause of any other' (247/1.4.5.30). So reason certainly can't help, and experience can't either. Experience is never going to make any constant conjunction less incomprehensible than any other, by allowing us to 'penetrate into the reason of the conjunction' (93/1.3.6.15). But then, if all constant conjunctions are equally incomprehensible, why pick on this one? (This is to put aside the worry that any judgement that something x is incomprehensible may be incoherent, on Millican's view, and so not really a thought at all—given that to say that x is incomprehensible is to say that we do not have wholly impression-copy-content-based or coherent idea of x.)

[13] These are the two main options he thought worth mentioning in his brief statement of his problem, although philosophers can obviously think up other peculiar possibilities (e.g. one persisting subject for every batch of ten or hundred of experiences, with observable 'real connexion' linking these successive subjects into a single person).

that the sea anchor of a correct interpretation of Hume's discussion of personal identity in the Appendix is the fact that he says that his philosophy could be saved if he could avail himself of either [O1] or [O2]—even as he acknowledges that he can't avail himself of either (his hopes vanish). The thought that he needs something like [O1] or [O2] to explain or ground [P3/P4], i.e. the evident connection among our experiences—or rather, perhaps, the thought that *there is no convincing response to someone who objects that he has in fact appealed to something like [O1] or [O2]*— is Hume's own thought.

3.3 Sources of confusion

The passage as a whole needs further discussion. For one thing, when Hume says that there are two principles he can't 'render consistent', i.e.

[P1] 'all our distinct perceptions are distinct existences' (so far as we know)

and

[P2] 'the mind never perceives any real connexion among distinct existences'

it's natural to read him as saying that he can't render them consistent with each other. But they're not mutually inconsistent as they stand, as is well known,[14] so the claim that he can't render them consistent needs to be examined. Confusion can also arise from the fact that [P1] is presented in straightforwardly ontological form while [P2] is partly epistemological.

Hume's overuse of the word 'principle' is another potential source of confusion; in particular, his use of it to mean not only a proposition of some sort, a theoretical principle of his philosophy, as in [P1] and [P2], but also—in the way standard in his time—a really existing phenomenon of some sort, as in

[P3] the principle of connexion, which binds . . . particular perceptions . . . together

or

[P4] the principles, that unite our successive perceptions in our thought or consciousness.

---

[14] See e.g. Kemp Smith 1941: 558.

With this in mind I will for a time write the word 'principle' as 'principleTH', where 'TH' stands for *theoretical*, when I particularly want to mark the point that it refers merely to a theoretical principle, and contrast it with 'principle^R', where 'R' stands for *real*, a real phenomenon, one of reality's 'principles of operation'.

This device allows one to say that the confusion is compounded by the fact that it is of course a principleTH of Hume's philosophy that there exist principles^R of the sort referred to by [P3/P4]. It is, for example, a principleTH of his philosophy that the principles^R of the association of ideas govern the succession of experiences in our minds. In fact there's a principleTH corresponding to each principle^R: the three principlesTH of the association of ideas record the existence of the three fundamental principles^R of the association of ideas (10–13/1.1.4). Note that this closeness of use means that there may not always be a single right way to take occurrences of the word 'principle' in the text.

Intense empiricists of the kind described on page 57 above may say that Hume isn't concerned with principles^R at all, objectively existing principles of working that govern what happens, but only with principlesTH, theoretical principles (like Newton's laws) that correctly describe observed patterns in the series of our experiences without positing any objective governing principles. This view can't survive an unprejudiced reading of the text (note that it will also have to apply to all expressions like 'influence on the mind', which was discussed in the last section), but one can for most purposes interpret Hume's references to the principles of the association of ideas in this way if one wishes. I'll say a little more about this later (p. 153).

There are, then, undoubted difficulties of interpretation. But if one stands back a bit, and considers the final two paragraphs of his discussion of personal identity in the Appendix as a whole (635–6/§§20–1), I think it becomes plain what Hume has in mind. His problem has the following overall form. It consists of

[a] the *initial problem* (how to explain or ground [P3/P4], 'the principles, that unite our successive perceptions')

[b] the *solution to the initial problem* ([O1] or [O2] would be enough, on Hume's view)

[c] the *new problem* (the fact that the solution to the initial problem is both needed and unavailable).

I'll now try to set this out in more detail. I'll use the expression *the I-Principles* ('I' for 'Imagination') as a general term to refer to the principle[R] or principles[R] that Hume takes to govern the operations of the mind and in particular the Imagination, which for Hume (see p. 57) includes 'the understanding, that is, . . . the general and more establish'd properties of the imagination', 'the solid, permanent, and consistent principles of the imagination', those 'which are permanent, irresistable and universal' (267/ 1.4.7.7, 1. 225–6/4.4.1–2).

3.4 The I-Principles

The I-Principles not only comprise the three fundamental principles of the association of ideas (Contiguity, Resemblance, and Causation) that govern the way our experiences succeed each other in our minds. They also and no less importantly comprise those 'permanent' and 'irresistible' principles of the Imagination (*sc* the Understanding) that lead all human beings, with the utmost reliability, to come to believe that they have experience of *real continuities*. What are these supposed real continuities, these objective-continuity-involving things that we come to believe we have experience of? There are three fundamental cases under discussion in Book 1 of the *Treatise*, physical objects, causation, and the self: genuinely persisting or continuous physical objects, genuinely continuous causal processes, i.e. processes which are not just a matter of one thing following another unconnected thing, and the genuinely continuous or persisting self. Hume's core theory of mental process doesn't just include

[P5] the Contiguity principle of association of ideas (e.g. an idea of one room may give rise to an idea of the room next door)

[P6] the Resemblance principle of association of ideas (e.g. thinking of a picture of Lucy may give rise to a thought of Lucy herself, or her similarly featured sister)

and

[P7] the Cause or Effect principle of association of ideas (thinking of a wound may lead one to think of pain).[15]

---

[15] These examples follow Hume's in the *Enquiry* (24/3.3). In the *Abstract* his examples are: '*Resemblance*; a picture naturally makes us think of the man it was drawn for. *Contiguity*; when *St. Dennis* is mentioned, the idea of *Paris* naturally occurs. *Causation*; when we think of the son, we are apt to carry our attention to the father' (Abs§35). It is important that these three association-triggering relations are relations between the *contents* of perceptions, not relations between actual perceptions themselves, although their existence is what leads one perception

His core theory also states that certain series of experiences of specific types give rise to certain other experiences which involve posits or 'fictions'. Specifically, and as just remarked, Hume holds that certain series of experiences give rise to ideas of, and belief in, *real continuities*. That is, there is a deep and inflexible principle of human psychology given which

[P8] certain general kinds of series of experiences give rise to the idea of continuing existence or identity.

We can illustrate [P8] by considering its three principal sub-divisions, distinguished by superscripts ('O' for objects, 'C' for cause, 'S' for self). The first sub-principle is

[P8^O] series of experiences of the kind specified in 1.4.2 give rise to the idea of continuing *objects* like tables and chairs.

There is a no less deep and inflexible principle given which

[P8^C] series of experiences of the kind specified in 1.3.14 give rise to the idea of objective *causal* continuities, powers, necessities out there in the world.

There is a third principle, no less deep and inflexible, given which

[P8^S] series of experiences of the kind specified in 1.4.6 give rise to the idea of a persisting *self* or mind.

[P8^O]–[P8^S] may be called the *real-continuity-positing principles of the generation of ideas*, for the best general description of them is simply that they lead us to believe in real continuities, and to take it that we have direct experience of such things. Really, though, they're just different aspects of one single great principle of the Imagination, [P8]: the principle which causes us to come to believe in real objective continuities when exposed to certain sorts of patterns of perceptions; the principle which causes us to come to have ideas (or so we think) of continuing objects and causal power and a persisting self.[16]

---

to give rise causally to another; I return to this point in 3.11 below. Note that the resemblance relation is special in that resemblance of content between two perceptions entails resemblance between the perceptions themselves.

[16] There's an illuminating sense in which [P8^C] only expresses part of what is expressed by a more general and more fundamental principle: the *necessity-projection* principle '[P8^{N-P}]'. For in the *Treatise* Hume strikingly traces both our sense of mathematical necessity and our sense of causal necessity to a subjective feeling: 'as the necessity, which makes two times two equal to four, or three angles of a triangle equal to two right ones, *lies only in the act of the understanding, by which we*

As remarked in 1.1 and 2.4 (pp. 9, 51), Hume has a normative use of the word 'idea' given which the mental items or thought-elements that I'm here calling 'ideas' don't qualify as ideas, because they're not ideas with empirically respectable pedigree, but only as 'fictions'. But he uses the word 'idea' no less often to talk of thought-elements that are not empirically respectable.[17]

There's no need to continue listing principles, but it's worth adding the principle or principles with which he opens the section where all the problems of the Appendix begin, 'Of the connexion or association of ideas' (1.1.4), i.e.

[P9] the 'solid' principles according to which human beings tend to form the same complex ideas, with the result that we tend to find words for the same complex ideas in different languages (see 10/1.1.4.1),

and noting, finally, that

[P10] impressions give rise to corresponding ideas

is a further, distinct principle central to Hume's general theory of mental process, whether or not it classifies as a principle of the operation of the Imagination. Taking 'idea' in the non-normative way described on page 9 to mean any mental element that functions in our thinking in the same general sort of way as legitimate ideas do, one might group all of [P5]–[P10] together under the general heading of 'the principles of the association and generation of ideas'. [P3] and [P4] are, I take it, names for the same thing, and [P5]–[P8] ± [P9]–[P10] simply specify the nature of [P3/P4] in

---

consider and compare these ideas; in like manner the necessity or power, which unites causes and effects, lies in the determination of the mind to pass from the one to the other' (166/1.3.14.23; for discussion see Strawson 1989: 156–60). On this account, we have two truly fundamental principles: a continuing-object-positing principle (covering external objects and the self) and a necessity-positing principle (covering both causal and mathematical necessity). Here, though, I choose to bring *object*, *cause*, and *self* under a single real-continuity-positing principle [P8]. One may say that [P8^C] is the form that the more general [P8^{N-P}] takes as applied to concrete reality, where it lines up with [P8^O] and [P8^S] as a real-continuity principle.

[17] 'Fictions' are mental elements that operate in us, in our mental economies, in our thinking, in just the same way as mental elements that qualify as ideas given the normative sense of 'idea'. See p. 9 above. One could call [P8^O]–[P8^S] the 'feigning' principles instead of the 'real-continuity-positing' principles, but the word 'fiction' and its verb 'feign' still mislead some who read Hume.

more detail.[18] [P9]–[P10] are not, however, relevant to the discussion of personal identity, so I will put them aside for the rest of this book.

We have it then, that [P3/P4] is/are the same as [P5] to [P8]. [P5] to [P8] specify the nature of [P3/P4] in more detail, just as [P8^O]–[P8^S] specify the nature of [P8] in more detail. They are, collectively, the I-Principles.

Hume's problem in the Appendix has most often been thought to be a problem with the details of his psychological account of how we come to believe in a persisting self in §§15–20, which cites three I-Principles: two of the principles of the association of ideas, [P6] and [P7], i.e. Resemblance and Cause and Effect, and the real-continuity-positing I-Principle [P8].[19] We can call this supposed problem the *Problem of Detail*, if only to say that it can't be Hume's problem. The first and crucial point is that he pronounces himself satisfied with his psychological account of our acquisition of the idea of a persisting self. Furthermore, when he tells us what would solve his problem he cites two forms of outright ontological unity or perceivable connection ([O1] and [O2]) that have no relevant bearing on the Problem of Detail. They have nothing to do with any *beliefs* about unitary or connected or persisting entities that we acquire as a result of the operation of the mind according to the I-Principles (e.g. beliefs in physical objects, causal connections, and single continuing selves).

Hume's problem, then, isn't the Problem of Detail (I will, however, return to this issue in 3.10 below). The best explanation of the fact that most interpretations have gone wrong in this way, perhaps, is that many commentators have started out from a prior commitment to a false view of what kind of empiricist Hume is that has left them little alternative.

---

[18] Hume also calls experience, habit, and custom 'principles'. 'Experience is a principle, which instructs me in the several conjunctions of objects for the past. Habit is another principle, which determines me to expect the same for the future; and both of them conspiring to operate upon the imagination, make me form certain ideas in a more intense and lively manner, than others, which are not attended with the same advantages. Without this quality, by which the mind enlivens some ideas beyond others (which seemingly is so trivial, and so little founded on reason) we cou'd never assent to any argument, nor carry our view beyond those few objects, which are present to our senses.' (265/1.4.7.3) '. . . nor is it from any other principle but custom operating upon the imagination, that we can draw any inference from the appearance of one to the existence of another' (103/1.3.8.12).

[19] For details and references see e.g. Garrett 1997, Ellis 2006 (Garrett agrees that Hume's problem is not the Problem of Detail).

3.5 Bundles are just bundles

Some commentators have suggested that what Hume realizes in the Appendix is that he is, on his own theory, faced with the great set of all experiences, as it were, all floating around independently, and sees that he has to give (and despairs of giving) an account of how to assign individual experiences to individual 'bundles' in such a way as to be able to distinguish one mind-constituting bundle of experiences from another. There is, however, no evidence that Hume took this to be his problem in this form. As Craig says, Hume takes it in 1.4.6 that 'perceptions arrive already done up into bundles and the apparatus of laws of association and the rest goes to work in each case on a *given* bundle' in producing the belief in a persisting self.[20] One's situation is that one is faced with a bundle of experiences which are already given as being members of a single bundle or 'heap or collection' (207/1.4.2.39) simply in being the experiences one encounters. Today we might say that the experiences in question are the ones we encounter 'from the inside' or 'first-person' point of view, but such a characterization is unnecessary for Hume, because these are the only ones we encounter at all on the terms of his project.

The illustrative case he introduces, when he finally begins to examine the precise way in which experience of relations of resemblance and causation produce our idea of personal identity, takes up a non-first-person point of view—

suppose we cou'd see clearly into the breast of another, and observe that succession of perceptions, which constitutes his mind or thinking principle (260/§18)

—but the idea is the same: a specific set of experiences, a bundle of experiences, is already given as a bundle, a single bundle of individually 'loose' experiences. The analysis of how belief in the existence of a single continuing mental thing arises proceeds from there: Hume points out that the individual experiences in the given bundle stand in many relations of resemblance and causation, and in this way give rise to the belief in there being a continuing single mental thing.

---

[20] 1987: 113. Craig is at this point characterizing a mistaken objection to Hume. Stroud 1977: 137–40 also notes and discusses this point.

The passage just quoted from 260/§18 occurs near the end of the page of the original edition of the *Treatise* to which Hume refers by footnote in the Appendix—

having thus loosen'd all our particular perceptions, when[1] I proceed to explain the principle of connexion, which binds them together, and makes us attribute to them a real simplicity and identity; I am sensible, that my account is very defective . . . [21]

—and the purpose of the footnote is to indicate the point at which he believes his account of personal identity goes wrong. This may be thought to support the idea that what troubles Hume is the fact that he helps himself to the idea that experiences 'arrive already done up into bundles', but this is a mistake. Hume's footnote reference settles nothing. This is because all it does is refer to the page on which he finally turns to focus on the specific case of personal identity in §17. It refers to the whole discussion of this matter, which occupies §§17–20 and contains the central statement of his position, already quoted:

the true idea of the human mind, is to consider it as a system of different perceptions or different existences, which are link'd together by the relation of cause and effect and mutually produce, destroy, influence, and modify each other.[22]

The footnote reference can't favour one account of Hume's problem over another unless one of them locates his problem in some part of 1.4.6 that isn't specifically concerned with his account of personal identity in §§17–20. What is crucial is that the problem begins precisely when, and because, Hume has 'loosen'd all our particular perceptions'. It is this loosening in 1.4.6, which he cannot possibly avoid, because it is the only empirically warranted account of the mind, which is the whole source of his problem. This, in fact, explains the placing of the footnote.

Craig, again, has a sure grip on the issue. It is indeed given, for Hume, that there are individual minds, and hence that experiences come in given

---

[21] App§20. The footnote reference number attached to the word 'when' is Hume's own. It refers back to p. 452 of the original text, which begins in §16 ' . . . if disjoin'd by the greatest difference' and ends in §18 ' . . . amidst all its variations' (in the Selby-Bigge edition the footnote refers to p. 260, in the Norton edition it refers to pp. 169–70).

[22] It's worth noting that the 'true idea' definition of the mind makes no explicit mention of the impressions of sensation that are constantly flooding in during ordinary waking life, even if they're always causally linked (if only as causes) to other perceptions.

bundles.[23] A mind has, in fact, an essential nature. The trouble is that 'the essence of the mind [is] unknown to us'. So we certainly don't acquire our idea of ourselves as single continuing mental things from any experiential encounter with the essence of the mind. So where do we get it from? Hume's claim, of course, and again, is that all we encounter in experience is a bundle of distinct and as far as we know entirely metaphysically separate ('loosen'd') experiences. It follows, for him, that the idea of a bundle of distinct (and as far as we know entirely metaphysically separate) experiences constitutes the whole of the philosophically legitimate or 'true idea of the human mind'. This, once again, is the problem of the Appendix. It's not the fact that experiences come in bundles. It's the fact that *the bundles are just bundles*. It's the fact that the bundles are indeed bundles, mere bundles, like bundles of sticks. Sticks that have been bundled together have no real unity; they've just been bundled together.

This is the point of the term 'bundle', or 'heap', or 'collection'. A bundle or heap, a mere bundle or heap, is naturally thought of as something which is such that there is no real connection between its members. This is why Hume's problem—the fact that his own overall theory of mind appeals to the idea that the experiences are *really* or *objectively* connected or united in certain ways—remains untouched even after it's allowed that experiences come already done up into bundles. His problem isn't how to get experiences into bundles, or how or why they come in bundles.[24] It isn't what one might call *The Bundling Problem*. The correct response to the fact of bundling is to say that that's just how things present themselves, the reason for this— 'the essence of the mind'—'being . . . unknown'. It's taken for granted. It's not up for discussion. Hume's problem is that he has himself assumed in his philosophy that the bundles aren't mere bundles, in such a way that he can't with any plausibility reject a certain general substantive metaphysical characterization of what a mind's being more than a bundle consists in—a characterization that his empiricism forbids.[25] He can't keep this general

---

[23] More simply, and as before: the fact is that each person, in coming to experience themselves as a continuing single mental thing, just is reacting to a given bundle ('each person' is shorthand, in the way explained on p. 36).

[24] This is Stroud's view of the problem (1977: 137–40).

[25] The problem of how to group experiences into individual bundles is indeed a huge (insuperable) problem for radical empiricist ontological-bundle theorists of the sort who existed at one point in the twentieth century. It's very well set out in Foster's discussion of Ayer's account of personal identity (Foster 1985).

substantive metaphysical characterization out of his *positive philosophical* account of what the mind is—his account of the content or meaning of the idea *mind*.

3.6 Garrett's objection

—This is all very well, except for one thing. Hume agrees that his account requires or presupposes something more than just a series or bundle of experiences (you yourself stress the point that he never endorses the outright ontological bundle theory of the mind). But this 'something more' isn't a problem for him. It's not a problem for him because he can treat it in the same way in which he treats many other things—as something not further explicable by us, something 'mostly unknown' that 'must be resolv'd into original qualities of human nature, which I pretend not to explain', something that is part of 'the essence of the mind [that is] equally unknown to us with that of external bodies', something 'magical' and 'wonderful and unintelligible' (i.e. not understandable) by us. (xvii/Int§8, 13/1.1.4.6, 24/1.1.7.15, 179/1.3.16.9)

This is a good objection, and it needs a response. It's raised explicitly, in one form, by Don Garrett, so I'll call it *Garrett's objection*.[26] Many interpretations of Hume's Appendix fail to take adequate account of the Appendix passage that is the sea anchor of any correct interpretation, i.e. 'did our perceptions either inhere in something simple and individual, or did the mind perceive some real connexion among them, there wou'd be no difficulty in the case' (636/App§21). This is true of all interpretations that think that Hume's problem is what I've called the *Problem of Detail*, a problem with the details of his account of how certain of the I-Principles ([P6], [P7], and [P8]) generate the idea of a persisting mind or self. Garrett's objection, by contrast, takes direct account of the sea anchor passage and directly denies that it has the importance I attribute to it.[27]

The principal difficulty for Garrett's objection can be put by saying that it seems to be an objection that must be put to Hume himself, because it's Hume himself who so plainly says that he has the problem that he doesn't have if Garrett's objection is correct.

---

[26] See Garrett 1997: 171. It's raised as an objection to Stroud 1977 and Beauchamp 1979.

[27] Garrett has changed his view about Hume's problem in the Appendix since he published *Cognition and Commitment* in 1997—see the next section—but he and I remain in agreement in this central respect.

All this needs to be explained. First, though, let me briefly rehearse a point on which all moderately attentive readers of Hume agree, in order to put it out of the way once and for all. This is the by now familiar point that Hume isn't an outright ontological bundle theorist. He doesn't think that all there is to the mind is a series of experiences or perceptions. He can't think this, for many reasons detailed in Part 2—if only because he holds that 'the perceptions of the mind are perfectly known' and that 'the essence of the mind [is] unknown' (366/2.2.6.2, xvii/Int§8). And he is, again, a sceptic—someone who doesn't go around claiming to know the ultimate nature of things (other than perceptions). His position is simply that the idea of the mind as a series or bundle of experiences is the only idea of the mind that can pass as clear and distinct according to empiricist principles of clarity and distinctness. So his problem is not the problem that faces those who are outright ontological-bundle theorists about the mind and then realize that they have assumed something more than that in their philosophy. I'll call this the *Non-Existent Problem*, because it isn't a problem that exists for Hume or any genuine Humean.

The next section is not part of the main argument of Part 3, and may be omitted.

3.7 Placeless perceptions?

I want next to consider and reject the proposal that Hume's problem in the Appendix stems crucially from his commitment to the view that some perceptions exist 'no where' (235/1.4.5.10). Don Garrett has recently argued for a view of this kind, and his work triggered the current section, although the proposal I'm going to consider is not his.[28]

According to this proposal, Hume's hopes vanish in the Appendix because he realizes that it's not possible for certain perceptions to enter into the sorts of causal relations they do enter into according to the bundle theory of mind ('as to *causation*, . . . the true idea of the human mind, is to consider it as a system of different perceptions or different existences' (261/ §19)). His problem is that he holds, or appears to hold, the four following inconsistent views.

---

[28] Garrett 2011. In fact his paper provides an answer to the current proposal.

[1] Some perceptions, e.g. olfactory or auditory sensations or moral reflections, exist 'nowhere', i.e. nowhere in space (235–6/1.4.5.10).

I'll call these perceptions 'Nowhere-perceptions' or 'N-perceptions' for short.

[2] Some perceptions, e.g. visual and tactile perceptions, are 'extended', and presumably therefore exist somewhere in space (236/1.4.5.10).

I'll call these 'Somewhere perceptions' or 'S-perceptions' for short.

[3] N-perceptions and S-perceptions can and do enter into causal relations, according to the 'true idea of the human mind'.

[4] For any cause and effect, 'the cause and effect must be contiguous in space and time'. (173/1.3.15.3)

[4] is the first rule in the section called 'Rules by which to judge of causes and effects'. This looks at first like a good explanation of why Hume's hopes vanish, because, whatever difficulties we may find in [1] and [2], N-perceptions can't possibly be spatially contiguous with S-perceptions in such a way as to be able to enter into empirically sanctioned causal relations with them, as the 'true idea' of the mind requires.[29]
The key passage in the *Treatise* runs as follows:

> . . . *an object may exist, and yet be no where*: and I assert, that this is not only possible, but that the greatest part of beings do and must exist after this manner. An object may be said to be no where, when its parts are not so situated with respect to each other, as to form any figure or quantity; nor the whole with respect to other bodies so as to answer to our notions of contiguity or distance. Now this is evidently the case with all our perceptions and objects, except those of the sight and feeling. A moral reflection cannot be plac'd on the right or on the left hand of a passion, nor can a smell or sound be either of a circular or a square figure. These objects and perceptions, so far from requiring any particular place, are absolutely incompatible with it, and even the imagination cannot attribute it to them. And as to the absurdity of supposing them to be no where, we may consider, that if the passions and sentiments appear to the perception to have any particular place, the idea of extension might be deriv'd from them, as well as from the sight and touch; contrary

---

[29] In [1] and [2], isn't Hume making the old, terrible mistake of thinking that an experience of extension is itself and *ipso facto* something extended and that experience of red (e.g.) is itself something red? He's not making a mistake, although the issue is complicated; briefly, he's operating with a certain conception of experiences according to which they are literally identical with their ('internalistically' conceived) contents.

to what we have already establish'd. If they *appear* not to have any particular place, they may possibly *exist* in the same manner; since whatever we conceive is possible. 'Twill not now be necessary to prove, that those perceptions, which are simple, and exist no where, are incapable of any conjunction in place with matter or body, which is extended and divisible; since 'tis impossible to found a relation[1] but on some common quality. (235–6/1.4.5.10)

I'll begin with some general considerations, then make some points of detail.

First: if Hume had been principally troubled by the fact that N-perceptions and S-perceptions can't be part of a single causally related bundle of perceptions, because they can't enter into spatial relations, and causation requires spatial contiguity, he could have said this in the Appendix in half a sentence. It would be incredible for him to make no reference to this supposed difficulty in his summary of his problem in the Appendix. Consider how tidily he summarizes the 'no where' view at the end of the section in which he discusses it: 'All our perceptions are not susceptible of a local union, either with what is extended or unextended; there being some of them of the one kind, and some of the other' (250/1.4.5.33).

Secondly: the spatial contiguity condition on constant conjunctions that constitute evidence for causal connection isn't fundamental for Hume, as Garrett, for one, points out.[30] Certainly Hume's first rule 'by which to judge of causes and effects' is [4] above: that 'the cause and effect must be contiguous in space and time'. This is a sound working principle for judging of cause and effect in everyday life. But when Hume gives it, he's just reaffirmed his correct and central point that, a priori, 'any thing may produce any thing' (173/1.3.15.1). Certainly constant conjunction 'sufficiently proves' causation, but to say that it sufficiently proves causation is to say that it isn't actually the same thing as causation.[31] And 'we cannot penetrate into the *reason* of the conjunction' (93/1.3.6.15). So, again a priori, 'any thing may produce any thing': we can't know that spatial contiguity is required for causation. We can and should take spatial contiguity to be a necessary part of constant conjunction when judging of

---

[30] See Garrett 2011. Why do I say that constant conjunction is *evidence* for causal connection, and therefore not the same as causal connection (contrary to the view that Hume is a regularity theorist)? Because this is how Hume himself puts it when he's being precise. For relevant passages see e.g. 4–5/1.1.1.8; 212/1.4.2.47. For some discussion, see pp. 26–7 above, and e.g. Strawson 1989: ch. 15.

[31] See e.g. 136/1.3.12.16 and 174/1.3.15.9.

cause and effect for almost all practical purposes, but we have no reason to insist that it's a necessary condition of causation when we speculate about the ultimate nature of things like mind and body: 'the essence of the mind' is 'equally unknown to us with that of external bodies'.

Hume develops the point himself, in a discussion of the traditional philosophical dispute about whether mind is material or immaterial which follows the 'no where' passage.[32] Summarizing his argument towards the end, he writes that

we are never sensible of any *connexion* betwixt causes and effects, and that 'tis only by our experience of their constant conjunction, we can arrive at any *knowledge* of this relation. Now as all objects, which are not contrary, are susceptible of a constant conjunction, and as no real objects are contrary;[33] I have inferr'd from these principles, that to consider the matter *a priori*, any thing may produce any thing, and that we shall never discover a reason, why any object may or may not be the cause of any other, however great, or however little the resemblance may be betwixt them. . . . (247/1.4.5.30)

This, he points out, sinks the common claim that thought can't possibly be the cause of motion, or conversely; for 'tho' there appear no manner of connexion betwixt motion or thought, the case is the same with all other causes and effects' (247/1.4.5.30).

It follows that

you reason too hastily, when from the mere consideration of the ideas, you conclude that 'tis impossible motion can ever produce thought. . . . Nay 'tis not only possible we may have such an experience, but 'tis certain we have it; since every one may perceive, that the different dispositions of his body change his thoughts and sentiments. And shou'd it be said, that this depends on the union of

---

[32] In fact the 'no where' passage already contains a commitment to the view that spatial contiguity is not a necessary condition of causation: see 237–8/1.4.5.12. Garrett 2011 also makes this point.

[33] Hume's footnote here refers to the section 'Rules by which to judge of causes and effects', which opens with the same point: as far as we consider the matter a priori, 'any thing may produce any thing. Creation, annihilation, motion, reason, volition; all these may arise from one another, or from any other object we can imagine. Nor will this appear strange, if we compare two principles explain'd above, *that the constant conjunction of objects determines their causation*, and *that properly speaking, no objects are contrary to each other, but existence and non-existence*' (173/1.3.15.1). Note that this use of 'determines' is either straightforwardly epistemological, like the two prior uses of the word 'determine' in paragraph 1.3.15.1, or (like the fifteen uses prior to 1.3.15.1) adverts to the fact that experience of constant conjunction of As and Bs (say) 'determines the mind' to form an idea of B (say) on seeing or thinking of an A.

soul and body; I wou'd answer, that we must separate the question concerning the substance of the mind from that concerning the cause of its thought; and that confining ourselves to the latter question we find by the comparing their ideas, that thought and motion are different from each other, and by experience, that *they are constantly united; which being all the circumstances, that enter into the idea of cause and effect,* when apply'd to the operations of matter, we may certainly conclude, that motion may be, and actually is, the cause of thought and perception. (247–8/1.4.5.30)

Again in the next paragraph but one

... all objects, which are found to be constantly conjoin'd, are upon that account only *to be regarded as* causes and effects. Now as all objects, which are not contrary are susceptible of a constant conjunction, and as no real objects are contrary; it follows, that for ought we can determine by the mere ideas, any thing may be the cause or effect of any thing. (249–50/1.4.5.32)

And again in the following paragraph, 'matter and motion may often be regarded as the causes of thought, as far as we have any notion of that relation' (250/1.4.5.33), i.e. the relation of cause and effect.

So here, even as he summarizes the point about N-perceptions, Hume repeats—several times—his fundamental claim about the extreme generality of the constant-conjunction requirement on causation, and he does so precisely while making the point that we can't rule out causal relations between immaterial or 'no where' beings, on the one hand, and material bodies, which are of course 'somewhere' beings, on the other hand. The essence of the mind is unknown to us. When we come to consider 'real objects'—which of course include perceptions—we should accept that 'all objects, which are found to be constantly conjoin'd, are upon that account only to be regarded as causes and effects'. The fact that N-perceptions and S-perceptions can't be spatially contiguous (although they can and do stand in relations of temporal priority and temporal contiguity) gives us no reason to think that there's something wrong with the bundle account of the mind. Nor does it give us any reason to doubt that the bundle account is the only account of the mind that is warranted on Hume's empiricist principles.[34]

The passage of argument I've just considered (240–50/1.4.5.17–1.4.5.33) is one of the most powerful in Hume's book. It is, arguably, uniquely

---

[34] Remember also that we have no reason to think that space is real considered independently of the content of perceptions; all we know the nature of are perceptions considered in respect of their content.

illustrative of the force of Hume's view about our ignorance of the nature of 'real connexion' (I think he particularly enjoys it), and the general point it makes would, I submit, have been one of the very first things to come reassuringly to Hume's mind, if he had begun to worry that the claim that the bundle account of the mind is the only empirically warranted account was threatened by the disparity between N-perceptions and S-perceptions. I conclude that his worry is certainly not the fact that N-perceptions and S-perceptions can't fulfil the spatial-contiguity condition on constant conjunction, and hence on causal relation.[35]

Note also Hume's characteristic 'ardor of youth' in shifting from 'If they *appear* not to have any particular place, they may *possibly exist* in the same manner' straight to talking of perceptions which do 'exist no where'. It's reminiscent of his shift from saying that perceptions qualify as substances according to one traditional definition of what a substance is (244/1.4.5.24) to speaking loosely as if it was established that perceptions are substances—while at the same time continuing to insist that the notion of a substance is utterly unintelligible![36]

Note next that Hume's claim that 'tis impossible to found a relation[1] but on some common quality' is not supported by the section to which Hume's footnote refers back (1.1.5) in a way that allows the claim to constitute a good argument for the impossibility of causal connection between N-perceptions and S-perceptions.[37] The argument that follows

---

[35] It's not strictly relevant to the present issue, but one might ask why Hume insists on spatio-temporal contiguity as necessary to all genuinely causation-constituting constant conjunction in the physical world. Why not merely temporal contiguity? The answer is that he thinks that it is only in the case of spatial contiguity that one thing is actually in a position to *do* something, causally, to another (I'm suspending questions about gravity); only in this case can there occur the 'real connexion' whose nature we cannot know anything more about. There is, otherwise, no reason for Hume to insist on the point. This constitutes another devastating blow to the view that Hume thinks that the causal nature of the world is just a matter of constant conjunction, although it won't be felt by those who have habituated to that view.

[36] Recall Kant's exegetical wisdom on p. 8 above, n. 17.

[37] One fundamental rule expounded in 1.1.5 is '*that no relation of any kind can subsist without some degree of resemblance*' (15/1.1.5.8). But, first, perceptions presumably strongly resemble each other just in being perceptions, whatever their differences. Secondly, the constraints on resemblance are extremely weak: Hume's reply in 1.1.5 to the objection that 'the relation of *contrariety* may at first sight be regarded as an exception to the rule' is to ask us to 'consider, that no two ideas are in themselves contrary, except those of existence and

in Hume's text, which I've just discussed, explicitly considers causal relations between both N-perceptions and S-perceptions and minds considered both as N-entities (immaterial) and as S-entities (material). The argument as a whole is, no doubt, and for sure, in Hume's terms, 'absolutely unintelligible' but it is also fully intelligible in our sense; Hume's unintelligibility claim, as observed in 2.4, is not what it seems to present-day ears.

In the passage quoted on pages 123–4, it seems clear that Hume imposes two singly necessary and jointly sufficient conditions on being 'no where', or rather on being such that one 'may *be said to be* no where'. A being may be said to be nowhere in the relevant sense if and only if

[i] it does not have 'parts...so situated with respect to each other, as to form [some] figure or quantity'

and

[ii] it is not 'so situated...with respect to other bodies so as to answer to our notions of contiguity or distance';

and given that *somewhere* is (exclusively and exhaustively) the opposite of *nowhere*, it seems that a perception exists somewhere if and only if it fails [i] or [ii]. There is, however, a difficulty, because although visual and tactile perceptions appear to exist somewhere, in failing [i], it's natural to take [ii] alone to be sufficient for nowhereness, and visual and tactile perceptions seem to exist nowhere by [ii].

If [ii] alone were sufficient for nowhereness, then it seems plain that all perceptions would exist 'no where', when considered specifically as mental occurrences, as in 1.4.6. And this seems a plausible thing to say, inasmuch as the succession of perceptions in the mind isn't remotely like anything spatial, whatever kinds of perceptions are in question, visual/tactile or not (and putting aside the point the Hume actually takes it that all perceptions are located in the brain—see 60–1/1.2.5.20 and pp. 98–9). There are, however, many complications here (e.g. the previous point depends on realism about objects in space). Some of them trace back

non-existence, which are plainly resembling, as implying both of them an idea of the object...' (15/1.1.5.8). In a passage in 1.4.5 already quoted, he writes: 'we shall never discover a reason, why any object may or may not be the cause of any other, however great, or however little the resemblance may be betwixt them' (247/1.4.5.30).

to the shifting between 'perception' and object' which Hume authorized for himself in 1.4.2, and which I won't try to unravel here.[38]

I'm not sure it's possible to know exactly what Hume had in mind. There's a persisting tension between his all-out external-world realism of expression, when it comes to external objects (not to mention his materialism), and his official view that they can't be conceived to be more than perceptions. This tension is active here. What matters for present purposes, though, is simply the fact that Hume has no reason to think that his philosophy will collapse if one part of it implies that there are causal relations between Nowhere-perceptions and Somewhere-perceptions.

3.8 Unity and connection, real and Imaginary

Back now to the bundle, Hume's single, given bundle, his irredeemably 'mere' bundle of experiences. His principal question in 1.4.6 is his standard question in Book 1 of the *Treatise*, applied to the case of the mind. It's the empirical, psychological question 'Which properties of this bundle or set of experiences give rise to the belief in a persisting self? What is it about these experiences, exactly, that naturally and inevitably leads each one of us individually, when we consider the set of experiences we are confronted with, to think of them as forming or being part of a persisting unity that we may call *a* mind, *a* self, *a* person, something that isn't just a bundle of "loose" experiences?' He answers, as is well known, by reference to certain of the I-Principles (two of the principles of the association of ideas, [P6] and [P7], i.e. Resemblance and Cause and Effect, and [P8], the great general 'feigning' principle that leads us to posit real unities or continuities of one kind or another beyond the available evidence. I don't have much to say about his answer (although see the next section), because Hume himself has no problem with it; his problem is not the Problem of Detail. He says he considers his answer to the empirical psychological question 'promising', and I'm concerned with the part of his theory he despairs of.

If the Problem of Detail is not his problem, what is? Start, again, with a given bundle, for this is Hume's starting point: a given bundle of

---

[38] Reid grumbles pertinently about this in his notes for 'Three Lectures on the Nature and Duration of the Soul' (1766/2002: 617–8).

experiences, a given mind (one's own mind) so far as one has any empirically legitimate idea of it. The experiences in the bundle are real existences
that succeed each other in time,[39] and they are, as far as the empirically
admissible evidence goes, objectively entirely distinct and separate from
each other: a mere bundle. But they're *not* in fact entirely objectively
unconnected, according to Hume's theory of mind. On the contrary: it's
'evident that there is a principle of connexion between the different
thoughts or ideas of the mind' (23/3.1); an actual, non-'fictional' connection. If our ideas were 'entirely loose and unconnected, chance alone
wou'd join them; and 'tis impossible the same simple ideas should fall
regularly into complex ones (as they commonly do) without some *bond of
union* among them, some associating quality, by which one idea naturally
introduces another' (10/1.1.4.1). This point now weighs heavy on Hume,
because it is the foundation of the Unanswerable Objection: the empirically acceptable notion of cause that enters into the 'true idea of the human
mind' leaves our ideas metaphysically loose and unconnected, but they are
in fact objectively connected, in a way on which Hume's whole science of
man depends.

How are they objectively connected? They're objectively connected in
being governed by the I-Principles, by [P3/P4], 'the principle of connexion', in the singular version, 'which binds them together, and [in so doing]
makes us attribute to them a real simplicity and identity', 'the principles',
in the plural version, 'that unite our successive perceptions in our thought
or consciousness'.[40]

Some may still doubt that Hume here commits himself to

[i] the experiences being objectively connected,

rather than merely to

[ii] their being experienced as connected by us in our thought about
them.

But this is precisely his problem. He does commit himself to [i], and he
does so precisely in explaining [ii]. He commits himself to [i] everywhere
in his philosophy, e.g. in explaining our belief that we have direct

---

[39] See p. 44 n. 24 for a comment on the fact that Hume also says that they may be
contemporary within a single bundle.

[40] 635–6/App§20. One could say that all the exegetical trouble derives from the word
'unite' and the way it has been misread because of the traditional radical-empiricist view of
Hume.

experience of persisting external objects and causal necessity ([P8^O] and [P8^C]) and in explaining the way in which people tend to form the same complex ideas ([P9]). It is, he says, '*impossible* [that] the same simple ideas should fall regularly into complex ones (as they commonly do) without some bond of union among them'. This bond must be a real bond, not just a 'fiction', a feeling of a bond.

I'll use the expression 'unity-or-connection phenomenon', or 'UC phenomenon' for short, as a completely general name for *all the various phenomena of unity and connection* discussed by Hume. We can then say that part of the difficulty of his text arises from the fact that Hume is concerned in a short space with two radically distinct types of UC phenomena. The difficulty is compounded by the fact that the two sorts of UC phenomena are closely linked, in spite of being radically distinct: one sort produces the other.

Our experiences themselves are real, concrete particulars, and the fact that there is a principle that 'binds' them together—the fact that there are principles that 'unite' them (i.e. the I-Principles, i.e. [P3/P4], i.e. more specifically, [P5] to [P8])—is as I will say an *objective* or *real* UC phenomenon, a UC_R phenomenon for short ('R' for real). As such it's wholly distinct from the UC phenomena that are generated by the UC_R phenomenon of the mind's operating according to the I-Principles, which I'll call UC_I phenomena for short ('I' for Imagination-generated).

What are these UC_I phenomena, these I-Principles-generated unity-or-connection phenomena? They're 'fictions', natural 'suppositions' (in Hume's semi-technical use of 'suppose'), natural 'posits' (in Quine's preferred term), natural hypotheses produced by 'feigning' (Newton's term), hypotheses that we firmly believe and that go beyond, are not warranted by, the empirical evidence. Physical objects as we ordinarily conceive ourselves to know them are UC_I phenomena.[41] So are causal necessities as we ordinarily conceive ourselves to know them. So is the persisting self as we ordinarily (or indeed philosophically) conceive ourselves to know it. They're all 'fictions'. But the fact that a mind's experiences conform to the I-Principles isn't a posit, a UC_I phenomenon. It's a UC_R phenomenon, a real fact about the world. It isn't any sort of 'fiction' that the mind operates according to the I-Principles. How could it be? The UC_R phenomenon of

---

[41] Quine speaks of the 'myth of physical objects' See p. 57 n. 46.

the mind's operation according to the I-Principles is the *source* of all the 'fictions'—all the UC_I phenomena—that Hume is concerned with.[42] Hume's concern to account for the UC_R phenomena that *consist* in the mind's operating according to the I-Principles mustn't be confused with his concern to account for the UC_I phenomena that we come to believe in (physical objects, causal necessities, the persisting self as we ordinarily conceive them) as a *result* of the mind's operating according to the I-Principles. The latter are fully accounted for by the UC_R phenomenon of our minds' operating in accordance with the I-Principles. To try to explain the existence of the UC_R phenomena that we refer to when we speak of the operation of the mind in accordance with the I-Principles by pointing out that the operation of the mind in accordance with the I-Principles gives rise to UC phenomena would be like trying to use logic to prove the validity of logic.

Consider again the words 'the principle of connexion, which binds [our perceptions] together, and makes us attribute to them a real simplicity and identity' (635–6/App§20). 'The principle of connexion, which binds [our perceptions] together' is a UC_R phenomenon. It's the principle^R/principles^R ([P3/P4], more specifically [P5] to [P8]), whose holding across a single bundle makes/make that bundle a single 'system' (261/§19). The UC_I phenomenon that concerns Hume in 1.4.6 is the product of the process of the operation of the principle(s)^R: the persisting self we come to believe in when we 'attribute to [our perceptions] a real simplicity and identity' as a result of the operation of the UC_R phenomenon of the principle(s)^R. The operation of the UC_R phenomenon 'makes us' come up with this UC_I phenomenon. Hume's problem concerns the existence of this UC_R phenomenon, i.e. the existence of the I-Principles; or rather, it concerns the use of it he makes in his philosophy.

3.9 Interim summary

By his own admission, Hume is faced with an inconsistency in his position. But the two principlesTH

[P1] 'all our distinct perceptions are distinct existences' (so far as we know) (636/App§21)

---

[42] As remarked in 2.6 (p. 57).

and

[P2] 'the mind never perceives any real connexion among distinct existences' (636/App§21)

that Hume calls inconsistent aren't inconsistent with each other (as everyone agrees). Nor are they inconsistent with his official bundle account of the empirically warranted idea of the mind. On the contrary, they drive it. What they're inconsistent with is the principle^R/principles^R mentioned in the preceding paragraph of the Appendix, i.e. the I-Principles, i.e.

[P3] 'the principle of connexion, which binds... our particular perceptions... together' (635/App§20; plural version)

or equivalently

[P4] 'the principles, that unite our successive perceptions in our thought or consciousness' (636/App§20; singular version).

But one can put the point equally well by saying that they're inconsistent with what [P3] and [P4] seem to presuppose, i.e.

[O1] 'our perceptions... inhere in something simple and individual' (636/App§21)

or

[O2] our perceptions are distinct existences, and 'the mind perceive[s] some real connexion among them' (636/App§21).

The trouble is that [P1] and [P2] rule out appeal to a feature of the mind that Hume constantly appeals to or presupposes in his psychology-philosophy, i.e. [P3/P4] (more specifically [P5] to [P8]), i.e. the I-Principles. [P1] and [P2] are inconsistent with the 'evident' fact, on which Hume's whole psychology depends, that there's a real (*not* Imagination-generated) connection among our successive perceptions of a certain kind. Hume thinks he can give his reliance on this real connection an adequate theoretical grounding if he can appeal either to the fact that the perceptions inhere in a simple individual something [O1] or to the fact that although the perceptions are irreducibly multiple, one can perceive a real (not Imagination-generated) connection between them [O2]. But [P1] and [P2] rule out any such appeal.

Put negatively as before (and this is perhaps the best way to put it), Hume's problem is that he doesn't see how to resist the objection that he can't sufficiently account for the existence and operation of principle(s)^R [P3/P4] unless he allows that one of the two proposals about the nature of the mind—[O1] or [O2]—is allowed to be correct.[43] And what this means, in effect, is that he has to allow one of the two—or the disjunction of the two—into his account of the 'true idea' of the human mind; for the resulting enriched idea of the human mind is the one he has in fact used in his philosophy. But he can't possibly allow them into the true idea of the human mind given his fundamental principles [P1] and [P2]. These are his dearest philosophical principles, and they debar him from allowing that the terms that [O1] and [O2] centrally employ ('real connexion', 'something simple and individual') can have intelligible (empirically understandable) application to reality within the sanctum of clarity which his empiricist principles mark out as philosophy's whole legitimate domain.

Another way to put this is to say that Hume sees that [P1] and [P2] can't be right, as applied to the mind. Or rather, he can see that the account of the mind that they permit isn't the one he's been using in his philosophy, even if (even though) it's the only empirically warranted account. In that sense, the empirically warranted 'true idea' of the mind isn't the true idea of the mind after all. Hume's empiricist project can't be completed because it fails to account for the mind itself. His theory is fundamentally flawed: it works explicitly with something that it officially holds to be unintelligible. This is the kind of thing that makes a person's hopes vanish. It's a problem of the right size.

One might say that what Hume sees is that his philosophy allows (demands, constitutes) a transcendental argument in Kant's sense, an argument of a sort strictly forbidden to empiricists. It allows an argument not just to the conclusion that there is something more to the mind than a series of experiences—for that is something he never doubted—but to the conclusion that the nature of this something more is *correctly and knowably characterizable in a certain metaphysically specific* (albeit extremely general) *way*: either as a persisting single something or as non-single multiple thing that knowably involves real connection in a way that is not knowable given empiricist principles.

---

[43] There are other metaphysical possibilities, as observed in n. 13 above, but I'll take it that these exhaust the options.

3.10 The Problem of Detail

So Hume's problem can be stated in a sentence. It isn't a problem about what sort of ideas of unity or connection the operation of the mind in accordance with the I-Principles can account for, it's a problem about the unity or connection that accounts for the operation of the mind in accordance with the I-Principles. Why, then, has it most commonly been taken to be the former, the Problem of Detail, a problem with the details of his account of how the UC_R phenomenon of the operation of the I-Principles gives rise to the UC_I phenomenon of the persisting self we think we have direct experience of? How does this misunderstanding come about?

I think that certain popular ways of reading Hume have buried the possibility that his problem can be anything other than the Problem of Detail. But Hume may also be charged with being insufficiently clear when he writes

having thus loosen'd all our particular perceptions, when I proceed to explain the principle of connexion, which binds them together, and makes us attribute to them a real simplicity and identity; I am sensible, that my account is very defective.[44]

This is his first statement of the problem he faces on account of the fact that his philosophy makes crucial use of the UC_R fact that the mind operates in accordance with the I-Principles (the problem that the idea of the mind he deploys in his philosophy exceeds the empirically warranted idea of the mind). But it's standardly read quite differently, in the way just mentioned, as expressing concern about the adequacy of the detailed account in 1.4.6 of how certain of the I-Principles (specifically [P6] to [P8]) function to give rise to the UC_I idea of the persisting self.[45]

Why is this wrong? Let me rehearse the point again. When exactly do Hume's hopes vanish? They vanish when he comes 'to explain the principle of connexion, which binds . . . our particular perceptions . . . together'; 'the principles, that unite our successive perceptions in our thought or consciousness' (635–6/App§20–1). But what does he mean

---

[44] App§20; for the footnote reference number attached to 'when', see p. 119 above.

[45] Stroud 1977: 127–8 and Winkler 2000 are among those who think that Hume's footnote reference back to p. 452 of the first edition (260/§§16–18) supports the view that his problem is the Problem of Detail.

by 'explain the principle of connexion which binds' or 'explain the principles that unite'? What failure of explanation does he have in mind?

He tells us. It's his failure to explain the principle of connection that 'makes us attribute . . . a real simplicity and identity' to our experiences. It's his failure, in other words, to explain the *existence* of the principle of connection that leads us to come to believe in a single continuing mind or self or subject; not to explain how the principle does what it does. It's his failure, in other words again, to explain the possibility of the I-Principles, two of which ([P6] and [P7]) interact with a third ([P8]), when we take our own experiences as our object of attention, and generate the idea—fiction—of the persisting self.[46] The problem is that he can't in his philosophy make use of the fact of the existence of (the I-Principles-constituted) 'bond of union' among our experiences without thereby appealing to—or rather, without being open to the charge that he thereby appeals to—something he can't appeal to: [O1], the idea of the mind as 'something simple and individual', or [O2], some perceivable or experienceable 'real connexion' between experiences. The failure is not a failure to explain how the I-Principles lead us to come to believe in personal identity. That explanation has, as he says, and as already remarked, 'a promising aspect' (635/App§20). The problem is not the Problem of Detail.

Let us grant that the passage taken on its own can be read in the way that the old, false view of Hume seems to require. Subtle philosophers have done so. They have found Hume immersed in the Problem of Detail, despairing of his account of how the idea of a persisting self arises in us, on the grounds that [P6] and [P7] combined with [P8] can't really do the job. The question is whether this is a defensible interpretation of what he thinks his problem is. Loss of all hope seems a strangely extravagant reaction to such a problem.[47]

---

[46] Remember that [P5]–[P8] simply specify the nature of [P3/P4]—the 'I-Principles'—in more detail.

[47] Hume later comes to think that Kames gives a better account of the origin of the idea of a persisting self. Reading a draft of Kames's *Essays* in 1746, Hume writes to Kames that 'I likt exceedingly your Method of explaining personal Identity as more satisfactory than any thing that had ever occurr'd to me' (1746: 20). I take it that here Hume means Kames's account of the origin of our idea of or belief in a persisting self—'man . . . has an original feeling, or consciousness of himself, and of his existence, which for the most part accompanies every one of his impressions and ideas, and every action of his mind and body' (Kames 1751: 231–2)—if only because Kames's further remarks (e.g. 'this consciousness or perception of self is, at the

The way to find out—once again—is to look at what he thinks might solve his problem. Fortunately, he tells us straight away. One thing that would do the trick would be (the right to appeal to) the existence of [O1] 'something simple and individual' in which our experiences inhere; another would be [O2], some perceivable or experienceable 'real connexion' between experiences,[48] perceivable or experienceable in such a way that *the deployment of the idea of it in one's philosophy when treating of concrete reality* is empirically warranted. Either inherence in a single thing or knowable real connection between multiple things will give him the resources to explain the thing he has just said he can't explain. We can, then, rule out the view that his (initial) problem is the Problem of Detail, as remarked in 3.4. For neither [O1] nor [O2] can help [P6], [P7], and [P8] (whose operation is not in question) do a better job in explaining our belief in a persisting mind or self.[49]

Again this is a somewhat backwards way to put the point. A better way to put it, perhaps, is to say that what destroys Hume's hopes is his realization that he can't meet the objection that he has in effect appealed to one of [O1] and [O2] in placing the I-Principles at the very centre of his theory of human nature, in making them the great engine of his philosophy. He has in effect appealed to one of [O1] and [O2], although he can't appeal to either on his own terms.

One could put the point by saying that the passage parses like this:

same time, of the liveliest kind. Self-preservation is everyone's peculiar duty; and the vivacity of this perception, is necessary to make us attentive to our own interest' (1751: 232)) are very close to Hume's own published views in Books 2 and 3 of the *Treatise* (see e.g. 317/2.1.11.4; 320/2.1.11.8; 339–40/2.2.2.15–16; 354/2.2.4.7; 427/2.3.7.1).

[48] Some connection which is not just an I-Principles-generated connection in the Imagination, and is, therefore, essentially more than the relation of cause and effect so far as we have any empirically contentful notion of it. (As remarked in n. 3 above, Hume's prime example of 'real connexion' is causal necessity thought of as something that obtains quite independently of any action of the imagination.)

[49] Doesn't [O2], perceivable real connection, help with the Problem of Detail? No. It adds nothing to the psychological explanation of our coming to believe in a persisting mind or self that's already in place (it wasn't needed in coming up with the 'fictions' of external objects and perceived causal power): all that's needed for the mind or Imagination to come up with the fiction of a persisting mind or self is that it 'slide easily' along a series of perceptions that are related by certain of the principles of association of ideas. It doesn't need to experience real connection. (It thinks it does anyway, as a result of sliding easily along the series of perceptions because of their relations of resemblance and causation.)

...when I proceed to explain [the principle of connexion, which binds them together], and makes us attribute to them a real simplicity and identity; I am sensible, that my account is very defective ....

The noun-clause inside the square brackets denotes the phenomenon which is his problem, the UC_R phenomenon that is to be explained (the [P3/P4] phenomenon, whose nature is specified in more detail in [P5] to [P8]). His problem is to explain the existence of the UC_R phenomenon that consists in the mind's operating according to the I-Principles. It is not to explain how [P3/P4] (in particular [P6] to [P8]), once in place, does what it does (it 'makes us attribute to [our perceptions] a real simplicity and identity'). For, once again, the two ontological solutions to his problem that he offers in the next paragraph can't possibly be construed as a solution to that problem.

Finally, one could say that the word 'explain' is misread. It doesn't mean 'expound' or 'spell out'—expound or spell out the details of how the principle of connection that makes us attribute simplicity and identity to our experiences does its job. It means 'account for the existence of': account for the existence and operation of the I-Principles given the resources of a strictly empiricist account of the mind. Hume's problem is to give an account of the existence of the principle of connection that does what it does, given his commitment to the view that the bundle view is for philosophical purposes 'the true idea of the human mind'. Can't be done.

A Garrettian doubt may be raised about whether Hume really has any such explanatory burden. It may be raised in spite of the fact that Hume himself says he does. I'll address this issue directly in 3.14–15, after noting another possible feed for the view that Hume's problem is the Problem of Detail (in the next section), and then varying my main claim in a couple of restatements which may appear to increase its exposure to the Garrettian doubt.

3.11 Type-token trouble

Consider again the three main principles of the association of ideas: the principles of Contiguity ([P5]), Resemblance ([P6]), and Cause and Effect ([P7]). These principles help to explain why our experiences succeed each other in the way that they do—e.g. why an impression with content A gives rise to an idea with content B, say, and not to an idea with content

X, Y, or Z. If we ask what entities these relations of contiguity, resemblance, and cause and effect are said to hold between, the answer is that they are said to hold between the 'contents' or 'objects' of the experiences that they relate. Illustrating the cause and effect principle of association of ideas in the *Enquiry*, Hume says 'If we think of a wound, we can scarcely forbear reflecting on the pain which follows it'. That's because of the operation of the cause and effect principle of the association of ideas. In the *Treatise* he puts it more generally: 'there is no relation, which produces a stronger connexion in the fancy, and makes one idea more readily recall another, than the relation of cause and effect *betwixt their objects*' (11/ 1.1.4.2) or, as we might now say, their contents.

This is the causal relation considered as something that links contents of ideas, content-types like *wound* and *pain*. It's important not to confound references to the causal relation considered in this way with references to the causal relation considered as something that holds between two concrete token experiences that instantiate the content-types in question, e.g. two real, concrete, temporally located mental particulars that occur when someone thinks of a wound and is then led to think of pain. This is because the causal relation that exists between two such concrete token experiences exists equally in the case of all three principles of association, Resemblance, Contiguity, and Causation, as Hume's examples make clear.[50] Hume is speaking quite generally about all perceptions when he says that 'the true idea of the human mind, is to consider it as a system of different perceptions or different existences, which are link'd together by the relation of cause and effect . . .', or that it is a 'chain of causes and effects, which constitute our self or person . . .' (261/§19, 262/§20). He's not just talking about the causal links produced by one of the three linking principles of the association of ideas—the Cause and Effect principle! All three principles of the association of ideas operate causally.

Although this is clear, it's possible that some commentators have blended together the two different senses in which two experiences can be causally connected: either the things they're about can be causally connected (wounds cause pain), or the experiences themselves can be causally connected (sight or thought of a wound causes thought of pain,

---

[50] The idea of one room gives rise causally to an idea of the room next door by the Contiguity principle. A portrait of Lucy gives rise causally to a thought about Lucy by the Resemblance principle. See p. 114 above.

the portrait of Lucy causes a thought of Lucy, the thought of one room causes a thought of the room next door). This is one way in which the type-token ambiguity in words like 'experience', 'perception', and 'idea' (noted in 2.2 above) can mislead.

I don't know whether this type-token ambiguity is in play when Garrett writes that Hume's project in 'Of personal identity' is 'to investigate what relations produce associative connections among perceptions sufficient *to make them count as* the mind of one person' (1997: 185; my emphasis), but it seems to me that Hume does not have any such project. If one alters Garrett's claim slightly as follows: 'Hume's project is to investigate what relations produce associative connections among perceptions sufficient *to make us in our ordinary unreflective lives count them as*' the experiences of a single, continuing mind or subject, then I think it is true. But then, I believe that Hume can be allowed to succeed in this project on the general terms of the *Treatise*.[51] I think he can be allowed to succeed on those terms—and so does he, in the Appendix—even if his psychology is by present-day standards empirically crude and suspect; and even though he later told Kames that he thought Kames's account was better. The relations that are in question here, however, and once again, are only the cause-and-effect and resemblance relations between experience *contents*. They're not the real matter-of-fact relations that hold between experiences as concrete mental particulars.

—Objection. If two things are causally connected, then whenever you get the one you get the other. But Hume doesn't think that the principles-of-association connection between a particular A-type experience, call it A1, and a particular B-type experience, call it B1, is like that. It's not true, on his view, that if A-type experiences tend to give rise to B-type experiences then whenever there is an A-type experience there'll be a B-type experience. The association of ideas is not exceptionless in this way; it is rather, as Hume says, a 'gentle force' (10/1.1.4.1).

Reply. The principles-of-association connection between A1 and B1 (whether it be a connection of resemblance, or cause–effect, or contiguity) is a 'matter of fact', in Hume's terminology. It's a connection between two real, distinct concrete entities, two experiences, and all such real-world, matter-of-fact connections are causal, on Hume's view. So he certainly

---

[51] By appealing to the following I-Principles: [P6] and [P7], the Causation and Resemblance principles of the association of ideas, and [P8] the real-continuity-feigning proclivity of the Imagination.

doesn't think that it follows, from the fact that there isn't an exceptionless connection between A experiences and B experiences (even in a mind in which a strong A–B association has been set up), that the connection isn't causal in any actual case in which a particular A experience, A1, gives rise to a particular B experience, B1. It is causal.

Is this compatible with the fact that the connections between A experiences and B experiences are not exceptionless? Yes. On Hume's (plausible) account the mind involves a vast number of associative propensities, such as the propensity to think of B after having thought of A, the propensity to think of Y after having thought of X, and so on. Each propensity operates in a complex causal environment that is constituted in part by the existence of all the others. The consequence of this is that few if any of them will show a character of exceptionlessness when considered individually. A thought or experience of an A may usually or almost always lead me to think of a B, but if I've just been thinking of a C, and am in an environment with salient properties D and E, then (other things being equal) a thought of A will lead me to think of an F. And so on.[52]

Causal relations, then, obtain between particular experiences, considered as concrete, temporally situated entities, as they succeed one another in the series of experiences.[53] And they obtain whichever of the three principles of the association of ideas is in question. The relation of Cause and Effect considered as one of the principles of the association of ideas that relates experience-content-*types* (e.g. wounds and pains) has nothing specially to do with the particular concrete causal relations that obtain between

---

[52] If questioned on this matter, Hume might say something similar to what he says in other contexts, i.e. that there is an exceptionless law there somewhere (with a *ceteris paribus* clause to cover glitches in the brain of the sort discussed in 60–1/1.2.5.20), although we don't know all the complexities (compare Davidson 1967). If the law were to be given a psychological formulation it would be something like 'whenever there is an A experience in overall complex psychological context PC14763, then there will be a B experience'. (As a determinist, Hume will find no conflict between this view and the claim that 'nothing is more free than the imagination of man' (*Enquiry* 47/5.1; see also 23/3.1).)

[53] I'm leaving aside, as Hume standardly does, the constant contributions to the series of experiences made by impacts of the environment (including our own bodies). It's obviously not a problem for him that experiences that are not in any way the product of the operation of the I-principles—brand new impressions of sensation—are constantly arising in the series of experiences. Note that these impression-experiences will almost always have strong resemblance, constancy, and coherence relations among themselves as they come streaming in, in so far as they have the character of being experiences of a smoothly evolving ordered external world; but this is another matter.

successive concrete token experiences, which are found equally in the case of Resemblance and Contiguity principles of the association of ideas.

3.12 Variation 1: the Identity Feeling

If we call our belief in personal identity (i.e. our belief or feeling that the self or mind is something that has some real diachronic continuity or unity) 'the Identity Feeling', we can restate the issue as follows. Hume doesn't have a problem with his account of how the operation of the mind according to the I-Principles produces the Identity Feeling, given that the mind does operate according to the I-Principles (something which is taken as given throughout the *Treatise*). In the Appendix he refers back to his account in 1.4.6 of how the I-Principles produce the Identity Feeling, restates it, and calls it promising, in the very same paragraph in which he says that something makes all his hopes vanish (635/App§20). So whatever that something is, it isn't his account of how the operation of the I-Principles produces the Identity Feeling given that the mind operates according to the I-Principles.

Consider the passage again:

. . . having thus loosen'd all our particular perceptions, when I proceed to explain the principle of connexion, which binds them together, and makes us attribute to them a real simplicity and identity; I am sensible, that my account is very defective, and that nothing but the seeming evidence of the precedent reasonings cou'd have induc'd me to receive it. If [A] perceptions are distinct existences, [B] they form a whole only by being connected together. But [C] no connexions among distinct existences are ever discoverable by human understanding. [D] We only *feel* a connexion or a determination of the thought, to pass from one object to another. It follows, therefore, that [E] the thought alone finds personal identity, when reflecting on the train of past perceptions, that compose a mind, the ideas of them are felt to be connected together, and naturally introduce each other.

[A] and [C] are [P1] and [P2], the principles that Hume restates in the next paragraph, saying that he can neither render them consistent nor renounce them, and we can reformulate the argument, particularized to the case of a given collection of experiences, as follows.

[A/P1] Experiences are distinct existences

[B] Experiences form a whole only by being connected together

[C/P2 + D] No connection among the experiences we observe is ever empirically discoverable by us. We feel there to be a connection among them, and this leads us to think that we do detect a connection, but this is because we mistake our feeling of connection for a genuine experience of connection

(this point is just a particular application of Hume's point about our knowledge of causation). So

[E] When we consider the experiences that are given to us as past experiences, we feel them to be connected, and thereby have experience that has the character of being experience of a continuing mind or self or subject or person. But we're wrong to think that the experience is, in having this character, veridical. For all we're actually encountering is our *feeling* that the ideas of the experiences are connected together, plus the fact that one naturally leads to another.[54]

This conclusion—that we have no genuine experience of a continuing mind or self in our own case—is of course quite contrary to what we ordinarily suppose, and Hume immediately grants that it seems extraordinary,[55] noting in apparent mitigation that there's a respect in which this account resembles Locke's account, which many of his contemporaries approve of.[56]

On that basis he concludes that so far everything looks fine:

However extraordinary this conclusion may seem, it need not surprise us. Most philosophers seem inclin'd to think, that personal identity *arises* from consciousness; and consciousness is nothing but a reflected thought or perception. The present philosophy, therefore, has so far a promising aspect. But all my hopes vanish . . . (636/App§20)

His hopes vanish when he realizes that the idea of the mind he's working with isn't sanctioned by his empiricist principles. It's true that the

---

[54] I don't think one would seriously misrepresent Hume's position in substituting 'the perceptions' for the words 'the ideas of them' in his version of [E]. Note that if one thought that 'naturally introduce each other' fell within the scope of 'felt to be', one would take Hume's claim to be that the ideas of the experiences are [a] felt to be connected together, and [b] felt to naturally introduce each other, rather than taking it as I do to be the claim [a] that the ideas of the experiences are felt to be connected together, [b] that they do as a matter of fact naturally introduce each other.

[55] He says something very similar in the *Enquiry* when discussing causation (76/7.28).

[56] The idea is that Hume's claim that 'the thought alone finds personal identity' parallels Locke's claim that 'consciousness makes personal identity' (1689: 2.27.10). The way in which personal identity arises from or is constituted by thought or consciousness on Hume's view is not in fact very like the way in which it arises from or is constituted by thought or consciousness on Locke's view (see Strawson 2011b), but Locke's view was already very widely misunderstood when Hume was writing, and, relative to that misunderstanding, the comparison offers itself as argumentatively neat.

empirically warranted 'true idea of the human mind' represents the experiences of the mind as 'link'd together by the relation of cause and effect', but it doesn't thereby present them as linked by a 'real connexion', because the empirically warranted content of the idea of the relation of cause and effect, as it features in the empirically warranted idea of the human mind, is just regularity of succession. Hume, however, is in his own view committed to a real link: it forms part of the content of the idea of the mind he is deploying in his philosophy even though it's illegitimate by his own empiricist principles.

3.13 Variation 2: the One and the Many

When Hume says that 'there would be no difficulty in the case' if our experiences inhered in something simple and individual, or if the mind perceived some real connection among them, he puts forward two options, arguing more or less as follows.

[1] Consider the mind of a given individual (a given bundle of experiences). The experiences of this mind are evidently *connected*; they're evidently governed by certain *uniting* principles. If they weren't, if they were 'loose', 'chance alone wou'd join them' (10/1.1.4.1), but that's not how things are. 'It is evident that there is a principle of connexion between the different thoughts or ideas of the mind' (23/3.1).

[2] How can this be? What must be the case, metaphysically speaking, if this real, non-'fictional' unity or connection phenomenon is in place—the UC_R phenomenon that consists in the operation of the I-Principles? What is an account of the mind committed to, in being committed to the existence of this UC_R phenomenon? It certainly isn't committed to any detailed account of its secret springs or mechanisms: 'the essence of the mind [is] unknown'. Nevertheless the commitment in question, the commitment to real unity or connection is indeed, and evidently, a *metaphysical commitment*. We're ignorant of the ultimate nature or essence of things, so we don't know what it involves in any detail, but there are nevertheless two metaphysical possibilities that are so general, and mutually exclusive, and effectively exhaustive of the field of possibilities, that it must fall under one of them. The first is [O1]: the experiences in question are united or connected because they all inhere in, or are states or modifications of, a simple individual something, a single object (when

the *unity* requirement is covered in this way, the *connection* requirement is *ipso facto* covered). The second, [O2], is that the experiences are not united in being properties of a single something, and are distinct existences, or distinct substances,[57] but are none the less really connected or united (i.e. not just connected and united in our Imagination) in some way we can't understand.

[3] We may take it that these two options—call them the 'One' and the 'Many'—are mutually exclusive and jointly exhaustive of the possibilities.

[4] Consider the One option: the experiences of an individual human being are not after all distinct existences but 'inhere in something simple and individual' (636/App§21). If we adopt this option in our philosophy we clearly have something that can ground the evident fact of the connection between these experiences. It doesn't matter that all further details of this something's ultimate nature are inexplicable and not understandable. The fact remains that we now, and crucially, have, in our philosophy, something that constitutes at least the *bare form* of an answer to the question 'How is the connection or unity between the experiences of an individual human being possible?' We're already committed to the existence of this evident connection or unity, this UC_R phenomenon, and although we can and should plead ignorance of the ultimate nature of things, we can't escape the obligation of acknowledging commitment to *the reality of some metaphysical state of affairs that can at least provide for the possibility of what we're committed to*.

[5] The One option isn't available in our empiricist philosophy, however. We can never perceive or (therefore) have any appropriately direct, philosophically legitimate evidence for the existence of anything like this (we can never have philosophically legitimate evidence for the existence of anything that is supposed to last longer than a single fleeting experience). This is [P1]. So far as we know, so far as all the evidence goes, 'all our distinct experiences are distinct existences' (636/App§21). The One option isn't available in our philosophy even as the bare form of an answer to the question of how something we're committed to—the evidently

---

[57] See 233/1.4.5.5, 634/App§12, 636/App§21. It's important that when Hume argues for this claim he argues only for the claim that they *may* for all we know exist separately. Compressions of the claim into its ontological version (as here) are a dramatic shorthand common to many empiricists.

existing UC_R phenomenon of the experiences of the mind succeeding each other in conformity to the I-Principles—is possible.

[6] That leaves the Many option, where the position is clear. If the successive experiences of an individual are indeed all distinct existences, and if we're aiming to specify how the UC_R phenomenon of their unity or connection (their conforming to the I-Principles) is possible in the most general terms, all we can do is assert that there is indeed some real connection between them—which must be empirically knowable, if it is to have a place in our account of the mind. For this is all we have left. This is the barest possible form of a positive account of the experiences' connection, given that they are Many. We allow, as ever, that our acquaintance with the fact that the experiences of the mind succeed each other in conformity with the I-Principles doesn't give us any knowledge of the ultimate nature of this real connection. We allow that it's inexplicable and not understandable by us.[58] We allow that it can't be specified in any further way than to say that it is indeed a real connection. This doesn't matter, because if we can appeal to real connection inside our philosophical account of the mind in any way at all, in however bare a fashion, then we will have something that can ground the evident fact of the existence of the I-Principles connections between experiences.

[7] But of course we can't appeal to real connection in this way. The Many-with-real-connection option is no more available in our empiricist philosophy than the One option, for we can never perceive or have any legitimately direct evidence for real connection in this sense. This is [P2]. It's true that the empirically warranted or 'true' idea of the human mind does represent the experiences of the mind as 'link'd together by the relation of cause and effect', but this is no help, because (as already remarked) it doesn't thereby present them as linked by a real connection: the empirically warranted content of the idea of the relation of cause and effect as it features in the empirically warranted idea of the human mind is just regularity of succession. But Hume is committed to a 'real bond' (259/ 1.4.6.16). He's committed to its being known, and *a fortiori* knowable, that the existence of the mind involves real connection, *however unknown the*

---

[58] Or 'mostly' so (13/1.1.4.6). Hume will happily allow the sense in which we learn more when we do neurophysiology, or improve our knowledge of laws of chemistry and physics, even while something always remains unknown.

details and mechanisms of that real connection are. He's committed to acknowledging this in his philosophy because he can't escape the obligation of acknowledging commitment to the reality of some metaphysical state of affairs that can at least provide for the possibility of something he's committed to: the 'evident' UC_R phenomenon of the experiences of the mind succeeding each other in conformity to the I-Principles. In the Appendix he sees that he has appealed to or presupposed real connection in such a way that he can't shrug off objections to his doing so by stressing the wonderful and unknown nature of the essence of the mind.

It's [6], perhaps, that most clearly reveals the central difficulty in the interpretation of the Appendix. In large parts of his philosophy Hume has assumed and fully allowed that there is real connection between the experiences of the mind in characterizing and invoking the I-Principles as he does. This assumption has been tremendously powerful and successful in allowing him to account for the origin of our ideas of physical objects, causal power, and so on. It's only when he turns his empiricist principles on the mind itself that he hits the problem. It's not obvious to him at first, because the I-Principles work just as well in accounting for the genesis of our belief in a persisting mind or self as they have already worked in accounting for our belief in persisting external objects and causal necessities (they work beautifully, on the general terms of the *Treatise*).

3.14 'Explain'?

—No. Hume can and does treat the 'UC_R' phenomenon of the existence and operation of the I-Principles in the same way that he treats other things, as something not further explicable by us, something 'mostly unknown' that 'must be resolv'd into *original* qualities of human nature, which I pretend not to explain' (13/1.1.4.6). The very fact that Hume uses the word 'explain' in the two crucial passages

when I proceed to *explain* the principle of connection, which binds them together

and

when I come to *explain* the principles, that unite our successive perceptions in our thought or consciousness

proves that your interpretation can't be right. For your interpretation requires us to suppose that Hume is lamenting his inability to explain something that he has repeatedly said he can't and doesn't need to explain.

This is Garrett's objection, somewhat extended. The best thing to do by way of reply, I think, is to start by considering points of agreement.

In operating in a way that is correctly described by the I-Principles, the mind delivers all sorts of unity-and-connection experiences, which we may call *UC experiences* for short. It delivers *persisting-physical-object* unity-and-connection experiences, it delivers *causal-necessary-connection* unity-and-connection experiences, and it delivers *persisting-individual-self* unity-and-connection experiences. Is the existence of such experiences problematic? Not at all. We can fully explain the fact that we naturally believe in these sorts of unity and connection, even if our basic experience consists of nothing more than a series of distinct and fleeting experiences, by appeal to the idea that the mind operates according to certain principles—the I-Principles—that generate such UC experiences. We can't, however, explain the undoubtedly real UC phenomena that we refer to when we speak of the operation of the mind in accordance with the I-Principles by reference to the operation of the mind in accordance with the I-Principles, any more than we can use logic to prove the validity of logic. So the fact that the mind operates in accordance with the I-Principles must simply be taken as a given (exactly as the conformity of physical phenomena to Newton's law of gravity is taken as a given).

So be it. This is what Hume does: the causes of the mind's operation in accordance with the I-Principles are, he says, 'mostly unknown, and must be resolv'd into **original** qualities of human nature, which I pretend not to explain'.[59] He could hardly be more clear: 'to explain the *ultimate* causes of our mental actions is impossible'.[60]

---

[59] 13/1.1.4.6. Hume would have loved modern neuroscience—although not nearly as much as Descartes.

[60] 22/1.1.7.11. In the same way, Newton states explicitly that he considers certain 'forces not physically, but mathematically: wherefore the reader is not to imagine that by those words [attraction, impulse, or propensity towards a centre] I anywhere take upon me to define the kind, or the manner of any action, *the causes or the physical reason thereof*, or that I attribute *forces, in a true and physical sense*, to certain centres' (*Principia* Definition 8); 'the cause of Gravity . . . I do not pretend to know' (1687: 3.240). Later on, of course, Newton *hypotheses fingit*, and decides that power has to be mental or volitional in some sense. Even prior to that, though, 'it was', as Hume says in the *Enquiry*, 'never the meaning of Sir ISAAC NEWTON to rob second causes [i.e. all causes other than God, in particular physical causes] of all force or energy; although some of his followers have endeavoured to establish that theory upon his authority. On the contrary, that great philosopher had recourse to an etherial active fluid to

Much is unknown, then, and must remain so. So far, Hume, Garrett, and I fully agree. And Garrett and I also agree—contrary to a cloud of commentators—that Hume does in fact appeal to real connections throughout Book 1 of the *Treatise* in appealing as he does to the I-Principles—to the 'uniting principle' or 'bond of union' that exists—the 'uniting principles' that exist—between our different experiences.[61] It is, furthermore, plain that the pre-Appendix Hume thinks that he can do this with impunity within his empiricist philosophy, because he can comfortably consign that in virtue of which the I-Principles exist to the 'unknown essence of the mind' in a thoroughly and indeed quintessentially Newtonian spirit.

It is at this point that the agreement ends. For I think, as Garrett does not, that Hume's hopes vanish when he sees that there's an objection from which this large confession of ignorance—this affirmation of ignorance—can't protect him. The affirmation of ignorance sweeps up almost everything, but it leaves a hole. Hume's position is vulnerable to the charge that if one relies on the idea of the mind's operation in accordance with the I-Principles—[P3/P4]—one is obliged to accept that one of the two maximally general positive metaphysical characterizations of the mind's nature ([O1] or [O2]) must apply. But to accept this is to accept that one must allow, inside one's philosophy, the applicability of terms that are 'unintelligible' by Hume's empiricist principles [P1] and [P2].

This is how [P3/P4], [P1] and [P2], and [O1] and [O2] relate.[62] Acknowledgement that one of the two maximally general [O1] and [O2] must be the case is compatible with vast ignorance of the nature of things, but Hume needs one of [O1] and [O2] inside his philosophy—there would then 'be no difficulty', as he poignantly says—for he won't

---

explain his universal attraction; though he was so cautious and modest as to allow, that it was a mere hypothesis, not to be insisted on, without more experiments' (73 n./7.25 n).

[61] 11/1.1.4.1, 260/1.4.6.16. Hume also mentions the 'uniting principle among our internal perceptions' at the heart of his principal discussion of causation (169/1.3.14.29), and holds that it is a matter of unintelligible real connection in just the same way as the uniting principle 'among external objects'. See p. 110 above.

[62] All six occur in the space of eighty-seven words (of which they make up forty-eight): '. . . all my hopes vanish, when I come to explain [[P3/P4]] *the principles, that unite our successive perceptions in our thought or consciousness.* I cannot discover any theory, which gives me satisfaction on this head. In short there are two principles, which I cannot render consistent; nor is it in my power to renounce either of them, viz. [[P1]] *that all our distinct perceptions are distinct existences*, and [[P2]] that *the mind never perceives any real connexion among distinct existences.* Did [O1] *our perceptions either inhere in something simple and individual, or* [O2] *did the mind perceive some real connexion among them*, there wou'd be no difficulty in the case'.

otherwise be able to 'explain' the I-Principles in the following highly general sense: he won't be able to account for how they exist at all, given that he has 'loosen'd all our particular perception'.[63] And in that case he won't be able to make use of the idea that they exist. But they're central to his philosophy. One might say that the trouble with his empirically warranted account of the mind is not so much that it doesn't contain [O1] or [O2], but that 'having loosen'd all our particular perceptions' (635/App§20), it positively rules them both out.

There's a moment when it dawns sharply on Hume that he has a problem. He realizes that the maximally general objection that one of [O1] and [O2], at least, is needed, and must in effect be allowed, given the notion of the mind that he has worked with throughout his philosophy, can be most powerfully pressed against him. I suspect that it was the idea of others coming up with this objection that was most vivid for him as he wrote the Appendix. One thing he then wanted to do—most understandably—was to be the first to make the criticism (think of Wittgenstein's assault on his earlier position). His best defence was to show complete candour and to be the first to describe the fork—the either-a-single-thing-or-perceivable-real-connection fork—that others would seek to spike him on. Imagine how you would feel, and what you might wish to do, if you discovered a serious difficulty in your just published and cherished theory. You would sit down and do something comparable to what Hume did when (probably hastily) he added the passage on personal identity to the Appendix.

One can put the point by saying that the existence and operation of the I-Principles mean that some metaphysical description of the mind that Hume can't avail himself of is knowably applicable to the mind. He can't invoke the mind's 'unknown essence', treating this as a kind of explanation-sink that can absorb the whole difficulty, for—this is the direct reply to Garrett's objection—his opponents can happily grant that of course much must remain unknown, while continuing to insist that Hume has in appealing to the I-Principles invoked something—some sort of genuine metaphysical connection and continuity among the experiences of the mind—whose existence he can make sense only on one of two conditions,

---

[63] To give an explanation of something *x* in this sense, to give an account of things that makes room for the bare fact of *x*'s possibility, is not to attempt any further detailed explanation of *x* of the sort Hume thinks is impossible and is happy to leave as unknown.

neither of which is available to him. Once again, one can say that the trouble with his empiricist account of the mind is not so much that it doesn't include anything that might satisfy either of those conditions as that it definitively excludes any such thing.

It's hardly impressive (it's hopeless) for him, faced with such an objection, to answer again that much is 'unknown', 'magical', 'unintelligible', 'wonderful', and 'inexplicable'. 'Yes, yes', his objectors reply in turn, 'we agree. The point we wish to make is much more general (it is, in twentieth-century parlance, a "logical" point). In relying on the I-Principles as you do you take a metaphysical step you can't take. You incur a certain general metaphysical debt you can't repay on your own empiricist principles. You can't rely on the I-Principles as you do and simply refer everything else to the unknown essence of the mind, for you can't stop someone replying that your reliance on the I-Principles entails that there is at least one thing that can be known about the essence of the mind and that you can't allow to be known. The thing in question is in fact an either-or thing ([O1] or [O2]), but that doesn't help. You can't allow this either-or thing to be known, because it isn't possible to specify what it is without employing terms whose employment you can't allow, given your brand of empiricism, when it comes to making knowledge claims about the nature of concrete reality.

'Specifically, and once again, your reliance on the I-Principles entails that the following high-level, either-or description of the "essence of the mind"— "persisting individual single thing or really connected plurality of things"—can be known to apply. You can't make room for this because you can't allow any empirical meaning or (therefore) concrete applicability to any idea of anything whose description entails that it lasts longer than a single fleeting experience. *A fortiori* you can't admit that any such idea has an indispensable employment in your philosophy, or that your philosophy presupposes that such an idea has valid application. But it does. Your philosophy entails—we're hammering the point—that we can know at least one thing more about the essence of the mind than you say we do or can: we can know something that we can't and mustn't claim to know on your empiricist principles. How else can it possibly be the case that experiences come clumped in groups that interact as they do?'

To this Hume thinks, quite rightly, I believe, that he has no effective reply. He can't say what he actually believes, given the dialectical context of his discussion of the mind. He can't say that the brain supplies all the needed real continuity. And even if he did, this wouldn't diminish his need to acknowledge real connection, for the brain is certainly not a simple substance (a property reserved to fundamental particles and immaterial souls).

3.15 Reprise

—You're seriously underestimating Hume's resources. He's 'not forbidden by his empiricist principles from postulating the existence of unperceived deterministic mechanisms that would underlie the propensities of experiences to appear in particular ways. He is forbidden by his principles only from trying to specify the nature of those mechanisms [in a way that goes] beyond what experience can warrant'. But he doesn't try to do this, in the case of the mind, nor does he think he needs to. He is, again, happy to say that what you call the 'I-Principles' are unintelligible, inexplicable, and wonderful. He has, therefore, no problem of the sort you describe.

This is another facet of Garrett's objection, mostly in his own words.[64] I think I've answered it. Hume doesn't think he can plausibly reject the objection that he's committed to something like [O1] or [O2], caught in the One/Many fork according to which one at least of [O1] or [O2] is correct (he's caught because it's a maximally general, exhaustive fork). [O1] and [O2] are very general, very unspecific, but when we consider the mechanisms to which Hume can legitimately appeal, while holding them to be unknown, we see that [O1] and [O2] already 'specify the nature [or ground] of those mechanisms' in a metaphysical way that goes 'beyond what experience can warrant'.

That said, let me repeat the point that the objection has to be put to Hume himself, because it's Hume himself who thinks he has a problem that could be entirely solved if he were allowed to make use of the idea of a simple individual substance, or the idea of (empirically observable) real connections. This is the fundamental fixed point, when it comes to the interpretation of the Appendix. It's Hume himself who judges (sees) that he is in effect committed, in his philosophy, to the allowability of at least one of two very high-level metaphysical descriptions of the nature of the mind that can have no empirical warrant and are therefore officially

---

[64] Garrett 1997: 171 (Garrett's text pre-dates, and is not a response to, any version of the present one).

excluded from any role in his philosophy. It's Hume himself who thinks that his empiricism allows him to ignore (delegate to the unknown, be agnostic about) all questions about the ultimate causes or sources of the patterns in our experiences that lead us to come to believe in physical objects and causal necessity, but doesn't allow him to do this when it comes to the mind itself. It's Hume himself who thinks he has a problem he can't solve even after he has stressed the unintelligibility and inexplicability of the workings of the mind—the mind whose principles of working are the great and indispensable engine of his whole empiricist programme—and who (again) thinks that he could solve the problem immediately if the principles of his philosophy allowed him to deploy the notion of a simple and individual substance, or to make empirically warranted use of the notion of real (non-'fictional', non-mind-generated) connections. The burden on those who favour what I'm calling Garrett's objection is to explain why Hume feels he has a problem he could fully solve if he could appeal to a persisting individual substance or make use of an empirically warranted notion of real connection. It's Hume himself who believes himself to be in a *Zugzwang*—a position where he would like to be able to make no move but feels obliged to make one (or admit that he has in effect already made one).

Old interpretative impulses may resurge: 'For Hume, the phenomenon of conformity to the I-Principles is brute regularity; there is therefore no need or possibility of any further explanation of any sort, however general, in his scheme.' The reply is the same. You have to contrapose: it's Hume himself who insists that it does need some further explanation or grounding, however general, and who tells us that two things that are completely unavailable to him would do the trick: inherence in a single substance or real—non-regularity-theory—connections. It is not as if he wants to say any such thing, appealing to notions whose use in philosophy he has ruled out as 'unintelligible'.[65] It's just that he believes (sees) that the objection that he must admit some such thing is correct and unanswerable. When he moved on from his empiricist account of the content of the idea of causation in 1.3.14 of the *Treatise*, and his empiricist account of the content of the idea of physical objects in 1.4.2, and took the idea of the mind itself

---

[65] Recall again that he uses them constantly in a way that presupposes that they do have content and are to that extent intelligible, and does not mean what present-day philosophers mean by 'unintelligible'.

as his subject in 1.4.6, his general 'reductive' empiricist account of the objective continuities (persistences and connections) that we take ourselves to encounter in experience was running beautifully. It was watertight on its own terms, and it must have seemed that it couldn't fail to deal also with the apparent or experienced continuity of the mind. And in a sense it did, and smoothly: it gave at least as good an account of the origin of our idea of ourselves as enduring selves or subjects as it did of the origin of our ideas of physical objects and causal power (which is not to say that it was in fact empirically psychologically correct). But—one more time—it's Hume himself who believes that his account of personal identity, his account of the mind, of the 'true idea of the human mind', is 'very defective', indeed hopeless, and that his problem would be immediately solved by one of two metaphysical provisions that his empiricist philosophy rules out.

3.16 Was Hume unclear?

Hume's account of his difficulty in the Appendix isn't really unclear (I've purposefully delayed the point until now). Entrenched assumptions have made it seem so (they have led many to think that his problem is the Problem of Detail), but these assumptions are unwarranted. The word he uses when he introduces the problem in the Appendix—'loosen' (635/ App§20)—directs us straight to a passage, early in the *Treatise*, that explains his despair, and that I've already quoted several times. Section 1.1.4, 'Of the connexion or association of ideas' begins as follows:

were ideas entirely *loose and unconnected*, chance alone wou'd join them; and 'tis impossible the same simple ideas should fall regularly into complex ones (as they commonly do) without some bond of union among them, some associating quality, by which one idea naturally introduces another. This *uniting principle* among ideas . . . (10/1.1.4.1)

The problem lies here. The trouble is that he has in his theory of personal identity, as he says in concluding his summary of it in the Appendix, 'loosen'd all our particular perceptions' (635/App§20). He's applied his strict empiricist eye to his own mind and found nothing but a heap or bundle.

Hume says that this is the trouble, straight out: it's precisely because he's 'loosen'd all our particular perceptions' that he can't explain 'the principle of connexion, which binds them together' (635/App§20). If ideas were 'entirely loose and unconnected, chance alone wou'd join them'. But they're not like this at all; they're governed by a 'uniting principle', the I-Principles. And the fact that this is so is the keystone of his philosophy—his science of man.

—Wrong. He hasn't loosened them unacceptably, because he holds that they're connected together by the relation of cause and effect.

It's too late to think that this response is any good. It's Hume's own judgement that his empiricist account of personal identity (according to which, 'the true idea of the human mind is to consider it as a system of different perceptions or different existences, which are link'd together by the relation of cause and effect' (261/§19)) is a theory in which he's 'loosen'd all our particular perceptions' (635/App§20) in such a way that he can't 'explain the principles, that unite our successive perceptions in our thought or consciousness' (636/App§21).

—How could he not have seen this earlier—or all along?

I'm sure the doubt was sitting somewhere at the back of his mind. But he must have been excited by setting out his empiricist account of the mind in 1.4.6, and there is a sense in which it works beautifully, given the explanatory resources (the I-Principles) with which it finally turns out to be incompatible. (Wait until something like this happens to you.)

—But Hume is already committed to real connection, and so doesn't really have a problem.

What he now needs is—as he says—*observable* and hence intelligible real connection. He needs what he can't have. He needs it in order to legitimate the notion of the mind he makes use of as a philosopher who, whatever else he does, can't give up the empiricism which rules out that notion of the mind as illegitimate.[66]

---

[66] For an expansion of the argument of this last section, and a somewhat different development of the main argument of Part 3, see Strawson 2011c: §§1–6 (§§7–12 of the paper summarize sections of Part 3 of this book).

References

Aristotle (*c*.350 BCE/1953) *Nicomachean Ethics*, trans. J. A. K. Thompson (Harmondsworth: Penguin).

—— (*c*.350 BCE/1924) *Metaphysics*, trans. with commentary by W. D. Ross (Oxford: Oxford University Press).

—— (*c*.350 BCE/1963) *De Anima*, trans. W. S. Hett (Cambridge, MA: Harvard University Press).

Arnauld, A. (1683/1990) *On True and False Ideas*, trans. with an introduction by Stephen Gaukroger (Manchester: Manchester University Press).

Aurelius, Marcus (*c*.170/1964) *Meditations*, trans. with an introduction by M. Staniforth (Harmondsworth: Penguin).

Beauchamp, T. (1979) 'Self Inconsistency or Mere Self Perplexity?' *Hume Studies* 5: 37–44.

—— (2000) 'Introduction: A History of the *Enquiry Concerning Human Understanding*', in *An Enquiry Concerning Human Understanding*, by David Hume (Oxford: Clarendon Press).

Berkeley, G. (1707–8/1975) 'Philosophical Commentaries' in *Philosophical Works*, ed. M. R. Ayers (London: Dent).

—— (1710/1975) 'A Treatise Concerning the Principles of Human Knowledge', in *Philosophical Works*, ed. M. R. Ayers (London: Dent).

—— (1710/1998) *Three Dialogues between Hylas and Philonous*, ed. J. Dancy (Oxford: Oxford University Press).

Biro, J. (1993) 'Hume's New Science of the Mind', in *The Cambridge Companion to David Hume*, ed. D. F. Norton (Cambridge: Cambridge University Press).

Blackburn, S. (1990/1993) 'Hume and Thick Connexions', in *Essays in Quasi-Realism* (New York: Oxford University Press).

Broad, C. D. (1925) *The Mind and Its Place in Nature* (London: Routledge and Kegan Paul).

Broughton, J. (1987) 'Hume's Ideas about Necessary Connection', *Hume Studies* 13: 217–244.

Buckle, S. (2001) *Hume's Enlightenment Tract: The Unity and Purpose of an Enquiry Concerning Human Understanding* (Oxford: Oxford University Press).

Burke, E. (1757/1990) *A Philosophical Enquiry into the Origin of our Ideas of the Sublime and Beautiful*, ed. Adam Phillips (Oxford: Oxford University Press).

Butler, J. (1736) 'First Appendix' ('First Dissertation'), in *The Analogy of Religion* 2nd edition (London: Knapton).

Carnap, R. (1950/1956) 'Empiricism, Semantics, and Ontology', in R. Carnap, *Meaning and Necessity* (Chicago: University of Chicago Press).

Cassam, Q. ed. (1994) *Self-Knowledge* (Oxford: Oxford University Press).

Castañeda, H.-N. (1966/1994) 'On the Phenomeno-Logic of the I', in *Self-Knowledge*, ed. Q. Cassam (Oxford: Oxford University Press).

Caston, V. (2002) 'Aristotle on Consciousness', *Mind* **111**: 751–815.

Chisholm, R. (1969/1994) 'On the Observability of the Self', in *Self-Knowledge*, ed. Q. Cassam (Oxford: Oxford University Press).

Craig, E. (1986) 'Hume on Thought and Belief', in *Philosophers Ancient and Modern*, ed. G. N. A. Vesey (Cambridge: Cambridge University Press).

Craig, E. J. (1987) *The Mind of God and the Works of Man* (Oxford: Clarendon Press).

Dainton, B. (2008) *The Phenomenal Self* (Oxford: Oxford University Press).

Damasio, A. (1994) *Descartes's Error: Emotion, Reason, and the Human Brain* (New York: Avon).

Davidson, D. (1967) 'Causal Relations', *Journal of Philosophy* **64**: 691–703.

Eddington, A. (1928) *The Nature of the Physical World* (New York: Macmillan).

Ellis, J. (2006) 'The Contents of Hume's Appendix and the Source of His Despair', *Hume Studies* **32**: 195–231.

Everson, S. (1988) 'The Difference between Feeling and Thinking', *Mind* **97**: 401–13.

Foster, J. (1982) *The Case for Idealism* (London: Routledge).

—— (1985) *A. J. Ayer* (London: Routledge).

—— (1991) *The Immaterial Self: A Defence of the Cartesian Dualist Conception of the Mind* (London: Routledge).

Frege, G. (1918/1967) 'The Thought: A Logical Inquiry', in *Philosophical Logic*, ed. P. F. Strawson (Oxford: Oxford University Press).

Gallagher, S. and Zahavi, D. (2008) *The Phenomenological Mind: An Introduction to Philosophy of Mind and Cognitive Science* (London: Routledge).

Garrett, D. (1997) *Cognition and Commitment in Hume's Philosophy* (Oxford: Oxford University Press).

—— (2011) 'Rethinking Hume's Second Thoughts About Personal Identity', in *The Possibility of Philosophical Understanding: Essays for Barry Stroud*, ed. J. Bridges, N. Kolodny, and W. Wong (New York: Oxford University Press).

Gurwitsch, A. (1941/1966) 'A Non-egological Conception of Consciousness', in *Studies in Phenomenology and Psychology* (Evanston: Northwestern University Press).

Hume, D. (1727–76/1932) *The Letters of David Hume*, 2 vols., ed. J. Y. T. Greig (Oxford: Clarendon Press).

—— (1737–76/1978) *New Letters of David Hume*, ed. R. Klibansky and J. V. Price (Oxford: Clarendon Press).

Hume, David (1739–40/2000) *A Treatise of Human Nature*, ed. D. F. Norton and M. Norton (Oxford: Clarendon Press).

—— (1739–40/1978) *A Treatise of Human Nature*, ed. L. A. Selby-Bigge and P. H. Nidditch (Oxford: Oxford University Press).

—— (1741–2/1985) *Essays, Moral, Political, and Literary* (Indianapolis: Liberty Classics).

—— (1742/1985) 'The Sceptic', in *Essays, Moral, Political, and Literary* (Indianapolis: Liberty Classics).

—— (1746/1978) Letter to Lord Kames (24 July), in *New Letters of David Hume*.

—— (1748/2000) *An Enquiry Concerning Human Understanding*, ed. T. Beauchamp (Oxford: Clarendon Press).

—— (1748–51/1975) *Enquiries Concerning Human Understanding*, ed. L. A. Selby-Bigge (Oxford: Oxford University Press).

—— (1751/1932) Letter to Sir Gilbert Elliot (10 March), in *The Letters of David Hume*, vol. 1.

—— (1753/1932) Letter to James Balfour (15 March), in *The Letters of David Hume*, vol. 1.

—— (1754/1932) Letter to John Stewart (February), in *The Letters of David Hume*, vol. 1.

—— (1759/1932) Letter to Adam Smith (12 April), in *New Letters of David Hume*.

—— (1776/1932) Letter to William Strahan (8 June), in *The Letters of David Hume*, vol. 2.

James, W. (1890/1950) *The Principles of Psychology*, vol. 1 (New York: Dover).

—— (1892/1984) *Psychology: Briefer Course* (Cambridge, MA: Harvard University Press).

Kail, P. (2007a) 'How to Understand Hume's Realism', in *The New Hume Debate* (London: Routledge).

—— (2007b) *Projection and Realism in Hume's Philosophy* (Oxford: Clarendon Press).

Kames, Lord (Henry Home) (1751) *Essays on the Principles of Morality and Natural Religion*, first edition (Edinburgh: Fleming).

Kant, I. (1781–7/1933) *The Critique of Pure Reason*, trans. N. Kemp Smith (London: Macmillan).

—— (1788/2004) *Critique of Practical Reason*, trans. T. K. Abbott (New York: Dover).

—— (1790/1973) 'On a Discovery', in *The Kant–Eberhard Controversy*, trans. H. Allison (Baltimore, MD: Johns Hopkins University Press).

Kemp Smith, N. (1941) *The Philosophy of David Hume* (London: Macmillan).

Kriegel, U. (2004) 'Consciousness and Self-consciousness', *Monist* 87/2: 185–209.

Kripke, S. (1982) *Wittgenstein on Rules and Private Language* (Oxford: Blackwell).

Locke, J. (1689–1700/1975) *An Essay Concerning Human Understanding*, ed. P. Nidditch (Oxford: Clarendon Press).

MacNabb, D. G. C. (1951) *David Hume: His Theory of Knowledge and Morality* (London: Hutchinson).

Millican, P. (2007a) 'Humes Old and New: Four Fashionable Falsehoods, and One Unfashionable Truth', *Proceedings of the Aristotelian Society*, Supplementary Volume **81**: 163–99.

—— (2007b) 'Against the "New Hume"', in *The New Hume Debate*, ed R. Read and K. Richman (London: Routledge).

—— (2009) 'Hume, Causal Realism, and Causal Science', *Mind* **118**, 647–712.

—— (2010a) 'Hume, Causal Realism, and Free Will', in *Causation and Modern Philosophy*, ed. K. Allen and T. Stoneham (London: Routledge).

—— (2010b) 'Hume's Determinism', *Canadian Journal of Philosophy* **40**: 611–42.

Moore, G. E. (1910/1953) 'Propositions', in *Some Main Problems of Philosophy* (London: Allen and Unwin).

Newton, I. (1687/1934) *Principia*, trans. A. Motte and F. Cajori (Berkeley: University of California Press).

Nietzsche, F. (1885–8/2003) *Writings from the Late Notebooks* (Cambridge: Cambridge University Press).

Penelhum, T. (1955) 'Hume on Personal Identity', *Philosophical Review* **64**: 575–86.

Perry, J. (1979/1994) 'The Problem of the Essential Indexical', in *Self-Knowledge* ed. Q. Cassam (Oxford: Oxford University Press).

Pike, N. (1967) 'Hume's Bundle Theory of the Self: A Limited Defense', *American Philosophical Quarterly* **4**: 159–65.

Priestley J. and Price, R. (1778/1819) 'A Free Discussion of the Doctrines of Materialism, and Philosophical Necessity', in *The Theological and Miscellaneous Works of Joseph Priestley*, vol. IV, ed. J. T. Rutt (London: Longman).

Quine, W. V. (1951/1961) 'Two Dogmas of Empiricism', in W. V. Quine *From a Logical Point of View* (New York: Harper and Row).

—— (1955/1966) 'Quantifiers and Propositional Attitudes', in *The Ways of Paradox* (New York: Random House).

Read, R. and K. Richman, eds. (2007) *The New Hume Debate*, revised edition (London: Routledge).

Reid, T. (1766/2002) 'Notes for "Three Lectures on the Nature and Duration of the Soul"', in *Essays on the Intellectual Powers of Man*, ed. D. Brookes (Edinburgh: Edinburgh University Press).

Rosch, E. (1997) 'Mindfulness Meditation and the Private (?) Self', in *The Conceptual Self in Context: Culture, Experience, Self-understanding*, ed. U. Neisser and R. Fivush (Cambridge: Cambridge University Press).

Rosenthal, D. (1986/1991) 'Two Concepts of Consciousness', in *The Nature of Mind*, ed. D. Rosenthal (New York: Oxford University Press).

——ed. (1991) *The Nature of Mind* (Oxford: Oxford University Press).

—— (2009) 'Higher-Order Theories of Consciousness', in *Oxford Handbook of the Philosophy of Mind*, ed. B. McLaughlin and A. Beckermann (Oxford: Oxford University Press).

Russell, B. (1912/1959) *The Problems of Philosophy* (Oxford: Oxford University Press).

——(1927/1992) *An Outline of Philosophy* (London: Routledge).

Shear, J. (1998) 'Experiential Clarification of the Problem of Self', *Journal of Consciousness Studies*, 5: 673–86.

Shoemaker, S. (1968/1994) 'Self-Reference and Self-Awareness', in *Self-Knowledge*, ed. Q. Cassam (Oxford: Oxford University Press).

—— (1986/1996) 'Introspection and the Self', in *The First-Person Perspective and Other Essays* (Cambridge: Cambridge University Press).

Smith, D. W. (1989) *The Circle of Acquaintance: Perception, Consciousness, and Empathy* (Dordrecht: Kluwer).

Stone, J. (1988) 'Parfit and the Buddha: Why There Are No People', *Philosophy and Phenomenological Research* 48: 519–32.

—— (2005) 'Why There Still Are No People', *Philosophy and Phenomenological Research* 70: 174–92.

Strawson, G. (1989) *The Secret Connexion* (Oxford: Clarendon Press).

—— (1994) *Mental Reality* (Cambridge, MA: MIT Press).

—— (2000a) 'Epistemology, Semantics, Ontology, and David Hume', in *Facta Philosophica* 1: 113–31.

—— (2000b/2002) 'David Hume: Objects and Power', in *Reading Hume on Human Understanding*, ed. P. Millican (Oxford: Oxford University Press).

—— (2001) 'Hume on Himself', in *Essays in Practical Philosophy: From Action to Values*, ed. D. Egonsson, J. Josefsson, B. Petersson, and T. Rønnow-Rasmussen (Aldershot: Ashgate Press).

—— (2003/2008) 'What is the Relation between an Experience, the Subject of the Experience, and the Content of the Experience?' revised version, in *Real Materialism and Other Essays* (Oxford: Oxford University Press).

—— (2008) *Real Materialism and Other Essays* (Oxford: Oxford University Press).

—— (2009) *Selves: An Essay in Revisionary Metaphysics* (Oxford: Oxford University Press).

—— (2010) 'Radical Self-Awareness', in *Self-No-Self*, ed. M. Siderits (Oxford: Oxford University Press).

—— (2011a) 'Cognitive Phenomenology', in *Cognitive Phenomenology*, ed. T. Bayne and M. Montague (Oxford: Oxford University Press).

—— (2011b) *Locke on Personal Identity* (Princeton, NJ: Princeton University Press).

—— (2011c) 'All My Hopes Vanish: Hume on the Mind', in *The Continuum Companion to Hume*, ed. A. Bailey and D. O'Brien (London: Continuum).

Stroud, B. (1977) *Hume* (London: Routledge).

Thiel, U. (1994) 'Hume's Notions of Consciousness and Reflection in Context', *British Journal of the History of Philosophy* 2: 75–115.

—— (2011) *The Early Modern Subject: Self-consciousness and Personal Identity from Descartes to Hume* (Oxford: Oxford University Press).

Winkler, K. (2000) '"All Is Revolution in Us": Personal Identity in Shaftesbury and Hume', *Hume Studies* 26: 3–40.

Wittgenstein, L. (1953) *Philosophical Investigations*, trans. G. E. M. Anscombe (Oxford: Blackwell).

Woodruff-Smith, D. W. *see* Smith, D. W.

Woolf, V. (1931) *The Waves* (London: Hogarth Press).

Wright, J. P. (1983) *The Sceptical Realism of David Hume* (Manchester: Manchester University Press).

—— (1995) Critical Review of *Hume's Theory of Consciousness*, by Wayne Waxman, *Hume Studies* 21: 344–50.

—— (2000) 'Hume's Causal Realism: Recovering a Traditional Interpretation', in *The New Hume: For and Against Realist Readings of Hume on Causation*, ed. R. Read and K. Richman (London: Routledge).

—— (2009) *Hume's A Treatise of Human Nature* (Cambridge: Cambridge University Press).

Zahavi, D. (2006) *Subjectivity and Selfhood: Investigating the First-person Perspective* (Cambridge, MA: MIT Press).

Index

This index does not cite every occurrence of every listed term or topic. Page numbers in bold indicate the place at which an entry is introduced or defined, or the main place at which it is discussed.